Singing Is Natural

by Jo Rainbolt

with voice technique by
Bonnie Jean Triplett

Illustrations by
James Erickson

askinelf

press

Dedication

Author Jo Rainbolt dedicates this book to her voice teacher and
contributing author, Bonnie Jean Triplett.
Ms Triplett's dedication is to her voice teacher,
Maestro Robert W. Knowles.

Acknowledgements

Thanks to Liz Fee for editorial assistance,
Michelle Edwards for cover design and typesetting, and
Ian Webber for musical notation. Publisher's logo design by Leif
Loseth, 82-year-old Norwegian fisherman from Petersburg,
Alaska.

Table of Contents

Part One Letting Go

by Jo Rainbolt

Part Two Vocal Technique

by Bonnie Jean Triplett

Preface

by Jo Rainbolt

I sang as a child and my mother remembers me as a singer but, still, I managed to reach middle age without ever having sung outside of the shower or on horseback. The act of singing had somehow become mysterious, reserved for a chosen few, even for a person such as myself involved in the not-so-ordinary vocations of writing and art.

Since receiving voice lessons for a birthday present a year ago, I have sung the black spiritual "Coming Home" as a duet with my voice teacher at a close friend's funeral and surprised my father by singing a song in Norwegian for Christmas, a language he has not heard since childhood.

Singing came back into my life at the right moment. I had completed an archival book on the history of western Montana that weighed in at five pounds, a job that paid little and demanded not only writing skills but those of editor, organizer, interviewer and photographer. A sense of tedium plagued me. Ordinarily I would have hiked into the mountains but a knee injury kept me from that; I was too broke to travel and my other pursuits—sculpting, drawing, gardening—seemed remote, even dull. And then, out of the blue, the gift of voice lessons.

Music is a language, it's not a big secret.

I went in feeling like a kid, eager for something new. When the teacher said lean-into-the-breath, I leaned. Since I couldn't read notes, I wasn't in awe of them. During that first lesson, I learned to let go and fly, to be brave.

The challenge came with language. My American diction insisted on chewing up consonants and shortening vowels. The a,e,i,o,u sounds we learned as children, so pleasing to the ear, are what make singing pretty, but I despaired of getting it right. A lifetime of pinching vowels stood in my way. When my teacher said "singing is speaking in musical tones, place the tones high," I tried to speak differently, but I still didn't get it, not until my third or fourth lesson when she put a Maori tape in the tape player in her dining room.

Shafts of sunlight came through the divided-light window and illuminated the polished table as I stood motionless and listened to the Maori's pretty voices riding on one breath, placed high, such ease. The community of voices floated through me and, as I continued listening, I recalled the convent I had walked past every afternoon on my way home from third grade classes in a new, seemingly hostile Nebraska town and the voices of the nuns, singing in sweet vowel sounds.

I went away from that lesson knowing these things: singing is a discipline that comes from within, it can be taught in the same way speech can be taught but only if we keep our speech high and our hearts open; that nothing is easier to take up and more rewarding than the art of singing.

PART ONE

LETTING GO

Santa and the Oldtimer's Band at the Salish-Kootenai Tribal Nutritional Center in Hot Springs, Montana, 1995. Banjo-player is Matt Olason; fiddlers are Hubert Marchbanks and Helen Spencer; pianist is Beulah Mae Marchbanks. Jacob Atkins is Santa and "Bluebird Joe" Parker, Center President, is sitting at the table.

Photo by Jo Rainbolt

Chapter One
Understanding Creativity

Jo Rainbolt's daughter, Kristen Schloemer, center, sings with kindergarten classmates during graduation in Hamilton, Montana, May, 1973.

Photo by Jo Rainbolt

Begin by Singing

"I used to sing," is a common statement, often said wistfully, as if the person gave it up to make room for better singers.

Could it be that we've been conditioned to believe that the arts are reserved for a privileged few? It wasn't always this way. Before the time of television and media-made celebrities, pianos were as common as today's home entertainment centers. People entertained themselves by singing.

Some became famous. Rosa Ponselle, daughter of poor Italian immigrants, began her musical career as a teenager in 1912 accompanying silent films in a theater in New Haven, Connecticut and, after Enrico Caruso heard her sing, played opposite the great tenor in the Metropolitan Opera where she continued to sing for nineteen seasons. I bring up Rosa, a legend among opera buffs but little known to the public, as an example of the spirit that prevailed during the early part of this century. There was no hype, she was a gifted singer, not a precious celebrity, and when she decided to stop performing at the height of her career she did it without fanfare and continued singing for herself.

The spirit behind singing is so much a part of my very being, that when I do sing, it portrays truth.
Faith Chosa,
a Crow-Assiniboine from
Hot Springs, Montana

In the 1970's, I interviewed people over eighty for a weekly newspaper column and found a spirit of nonconformity among those who had survived hardships and calamities with nothing to fall back on but grit and humor. I wasn't interviewing them as artists but as ordinary human beings who had survived rigorous lives, but still, I found they all had a form of self expression—oil painting, fiddling, weaving, quilting and, most of all, singing.

The morning stars sang together, and all the sons and daughters of God shouted for joy.
from the Book of Job

Sitting at a kitchen table covered with oil cloth and coffee stains, I've heard exquisite Irish ballads sung a cappella by an old miner. Another old-timer, a retired rodeo rider, demonstrated yodeling in a coffee shop and told me he couldn't sing Amazing Grace without crying because it reminded him of his deceased mother. A ninety year old woman played a honky tonk tune on her piano with her dog singing along.

I heard an Angel singing, When the day was springing, "Mercy, Pity, Peace Is the world's release."
William Blake

Music has always been used for healing in primitive cultures...harmonious sounds alleviate stress, and stress is the root of much illness, physical and mental.

Jessica Baron Turner,
musical educator and author

If you could trace somebody on a piece of paper, the outline of who they really are could be music. In my case, it is a reflection of the best part of being here on Earth at this time,

Guitar artist Pat Metheny

Visit a senior citizen center and most likely there will be a piano, someone to play it and more than a few singers. People who lived through the Depression had to entertain themselves. The American dream in those days was to do something, not to have something.

Look at any magazine cover or self-help section in a bookstore and it is made obvious that along the road to material comfort we have lost our sense of self. The more mechanized our jobs and lives become, the more we long for self expression. Who should we blame? The media for dictating which entertainers are worthy of attention? The ad men for selling us on more goods and services?

Why blame? It won't help get back what we've lost.

Let's begin by singing.

Letting Go

Singing is probably the oldest, deepest and most accessible form of human expression—no mess, no fuss, no supplies, just you and your voice. We were made to sing. Listen to the lyrical sounds a baby makes before speech. We find ourselves so delighted by this communication that we answer back in a lyrical way. Baby talk is singing. We had to be taught to speak but we were born knowing how to sing.

Still, we use our voices to speak, not to sing, and to do anything new or different requires a leap of faith. When's the last time you took a leap?

Most of us have to go back to our younger selves. Remember waiting to jump on the moving merry go round at the right moment during school recess? Or leaping into the center of a long jump rope held by two classmates? Sometimes a double jump rope? Even the most timid children have moments of letting go. Learning to read requires a leap of faith. Remember when fractions finally made sense? Those numbers we knew so well could become something else. Imagine being forced to learn that as an adult. I climbed trees to the top and outran boys as a child, but my favorite letting go experience was the afternoon I taught myself to swim in a Wisconsin lake. One moment my feet touched the familiar sand and the next I was over my chin and had to sink or swim. I suppose I did a hasty dog paddle, I can't recall the stroke, but I do remember the delicious feeling of I-can-do-this. Grown-ups were picnicking within earshot, but I kept quiet and practiced in secret until I could trust the fact, that yes, I could do it whenever I wanted, or needed.

As children, we all practiced such solitary acts. Since we weren't concerned with conventional society (at least not until a certain age) such communion with self was as easy as breathing. We accepted it as natural and were seldom lonely because we were in touch with ourselves.

Through singing, we are carried towards a simple awareness that many of us have not experienced since childhood, not the thrill of performing but an awareness that comes from within.

Overcoming Fear

If the idea of singing makes you sweat, put the idea aside. Doing it will be an entirely different matter. As with all mind-altering activities, the physical act—whether it be singing, sewing, sitting down to the blank page—is the catalyst that gets us into that elusive mental and emotional part of ourselves, the creative.

The creative part of ourselves defies explanation simply because it is creative. It might be described as inky, chaotic, unpredictable, flowing, scary, pleasurable. The poet Robert Bly likened it to a wet frog skin that a beautiful woman wore to conceal herself. You can imagine the consequences when her lover cannily removed it. Science has in the past decade or so attempted to give creativity substance through studies involving the left and right side of the brain. Our brains are double. Animals

Why not imagine the child's world as perfectly valid and complete, not something we grow out of or develop from, but one that we fall out of and forget. Could it be that in becoming adults we are educated away from the soul that is so vividly present in childhood?
Author Thomas Moore in a newspaper interview

When you think performing is the goal, you ruin the joy. The real focus is—can a person open up to themselves and sing for the pure joy of it?
Nicki Pisano, voice teacher from Missoula, Montana

...music is very difficult to define. It reminds us of who we were before and where we are going after. It is a mysterious vapor that somehow slips in the cracks between this plane of existence and some other one.

Pat Metheny

You stand up and start singing and forget all else. It's good therapy.
Arthur Argo
Hot Springs rancher, realtor and
beginning voice student

also have two hemispheres to their brains, but the halves work together. Our two halves are different as night and day. We might perceive of ourselves as one person but each side of our brain perceives life and processes information in its own way.

Scientists have only studied the right/left phenomena for a few decades, but it's not news—artists and philosophers have long alluded to the mystical side of human nature, and I have among my acquaintance Indian elders who grew up in what could be called a right-brained society. The intellectual left (or analytical side) has long been dominant in our thinking society but the intuitive right (or creative side) has gained immense favor in recent years. It is okay to be right-brained. The terms are batted around in everyday conversation, the actual studies are fascinating and almost impossible for the nonscientist to keep up. A good description of how the right and left side of the brain operate is found in "Drawing on the Right Side of the Brain" by Betty Edwards. In many passages, the word "drawing" could be replaced with "singing" since they are both skills that involve our mental, physical and emotional selves; and can be learned by looking at things in a different way.

To repeat myself, learning to sing requires us to create conditions where we can make the shift to the altered state. The desire is already there or you wouldn't be reading this book.

The Altered State

I experience the same fluid state of mind while singing as I do when writing or doing art. I feel awake and focused, but time loses meaning. Thoughts which come into my head leave gently. One beginning voice student describes the feeling as "open and at home with myself."

This altered state is not limited to artistic pursuits. It can happen during common activities such as driving, especially if conditions are familiar and pleasant. Listening to music, walking, jogging and meditation might also bring about a pleasant shift in consciousness. Reading transports some people, but being pushed into a class for the purpose of "bettering yourself" or reading books designed to "get you there" won't work. TV? Sorry, but TV is a trickster, a mind-numbing habit.

The frame of mind I am alluding to might be described as being out of the world but into oneself, as mentioned a few pages ago while discussing the focused activities of young children.

If the action is shared, or makes us anxious, it does not shift our consciousness. What works for some doesn't work for others. Hiking alone into the woods puts me into a relaxed, creative state of mind whereas driving of any kind makes me jumpy. Time might be suspended while I'm baking bread but the thought of making a pie brings to mind the Monopoly card "go directly to jail."

Singing Naturally

All this analysis of singing can make it seem contrived. It is time, once again, to remind ourselves that singing is a natural function that we have unlearned. The Old Italian method of singing which will be introduced in the next chapter is as natural as breathing.

If we give it some thought, we have all come upon a natural singer at one time or another. Mexico is full of them and so are black churches. It's been my experience that such singers are usually amateurs. The college dictionary I've depended on since the 1960's has several definitions for amateur, including "a person who engages in an activity for pleasure rather than financial benefit" and "a lover or devotee of an art, activity, etc." Still, the word often comes across as negative, perhaps we confuse it with amateurish, the next word in my dictionary, with only one definition: "characteristic of an amateur, esp. in having faults or deficiencies." I tend to stay away from labels (who says professionals can't sing for the joy and amateurs can't make

It's a fact, you cannot sing and stay grumpy.
Lynda Schmiedbauer
A soprano from
Hot Springs, Montana

Singing is a life thing, a natural part of being human.
Nicki Pisano

We are our own teachers. Once we learn the technique, we end up sounding like ourselves. Under the influence of a bad teacher, everyone sounds (or paints or thinks) the same.
Bonnie Jean Triplett
Hot Springs, Montana
voice teacher

"BURY ME A BONE ON THE LONE PRAIRIE-"

Music goes beyond language and beyond race, country or nationality. We recognize it as something we all have in common..the same thing you find wherever there is love, intensity, energy or human potential.

Pat Metheny

money?) but this one is interesting since it can taint our joy. Perhaps we should just think of ourselves as singers, or not think of ourselves at all but simply do it.

Back to my topic, singing naturally. Just the other night, I heard a young girl on public radio's Prairie Home Companion sing "Somewhere Over the Rainbow." Her singing was so effortless and free that, listening to her, I was over that rainbow. That's what I mean by natural: the voice is totally unforced, no choppiness of breath, no dramatics. While listening to such singers, we feel as relaxed as they sound. If practiced, the technique we are presenting in this book leads to natural singing. As I mentioned earlier, whole societies are born to it. But not ours.

Still, there are individuals born to it. When we come across one, we want to hear that person again and again. The natural singer I will be returning to as an example of how-to-do-it is Kenny Trowbridge. Born in Iowa in 1912, he followed his chuck wagon cook father west as a kid and was in his seventies when I heard him sing "Zebra Dunn" at his kitchen table. By that time, he'd retired to his armchair and was living on memories, but Montana's folklorist Michael Korn and I tape recorded him for a record "When The Work's All Done This Fall" and Kenny went on to become a nationally-acclaimed storyteller and singer.

The first lesson we can learn from Kenny is to not take ourselves too seriously. Kenny reflected in song and story what the cowhand loved best—the ability to laugh at life. We fear looking foolish when we try something new. It's okay to be foolish sometimes. Let's keep that in mind as we learn to sing.

Singing Families

When my partner of nine years and I moved to Hot Springs, Montana, he introduced the first cello. There was already a voice teacher, a number of musicians and (important for me as a writer) a woman who could read manuscripts with an astute eye. This woman who could edit also turned out to be a singer. Liz Fee came from a singing family. I'd met and envied such folks while researching Montana cowboy songs and fiddling tunes. One silver-haired gentleman told me that when he was a toddler, his father would crawl into his handmade wooden bed (a large crib with sides on it) and the two of them would listen to the Grand Ole Opry on the radio. Liz grew up picking out harmonies to go along with her two older brothers (one an excellent tenor). She sang with dance bands and was lucky enough to have another natural singer for a college roommate. They sang all the time. Imagine harmonizing your way through college. The two of them sang together as young mothers and keep in touch as grandmothers. Liz's astounding range dropped to the lower registers after a thyroid operation a dozen years ago, but there's nobody who can belt out a song with as much verve.

Just as it's never too late to learn to sing, it's never too late to become a singing family. My kids are grown up, but they've all taken a renewed interest in song since I started singing. Kim, my stepdaughter in California sings songs to me over the phone (and I sing back). My youngest daughter, Kristen, requested voice lessons for Christmas.

Spread the word.

Making a Song Belong

Andre Floyd is big, black and barrel-chested, a guy who can pick you up off your feet with a bear hug. A natural singer and a professional, he's settled back in Missoula after a decade or so of doing gigs in Chicago and other populated areas, and I'd easily travel the distance between me and Missoula (seventy bumpy miles) to get a hug from Andre, and heaven knows how far I'd go to hear him sing his blues and play his steel guitar.

It was a sunny morning in April when I ran into Andre at a college hangout in Missoula. He and two members of his new

When you sing from the heart and believe in the song, it becomes a reality and a part of what you are is given to others.

Faith Chosa

My mom used to talk about farm families in Missouri in the 1910's and '20's--how they'd dance and sing and play cards. That's all they had for entertainment. I grew up singing and married a fellow who sang. Hugh and I used to do duets at weddings and youth groups and our two girls grew up singing.

Virginia Butler, terrific pianist for local events

9

band, a harmonica player and guitarist, and two girlfriends were the only people eating breakfast outside. It was the first real day of spring with temperatures promised in the seventies but, still, this is Montana and it had frosted hard the night before. "Join us, it's cold out here," Andre hollered, and indeed everyone at his table except Andre looked half-frozen. He grew up in gusty Great Falls, a military brat, and cold weather doesn't seem to faze him (neither do the stares of whites not used to blacks). In the year since I'd seen him, Andre had opened his own state-of-the-art recording studio. The band was enroute to a jam session. Over a final cup of coffee, I asked Andre if he warmed up before singing.

"I do it by talking."

"I suppose that would work," I replied, "If you keep your tones high."

"Tones high, yup, and palate soft."

"Palate soft." That wasn't advice I'd heard from any other singer, including my voice teacher and Lamperti, but it made perfect sense. I wanted to hear more from Andre. We'd all completed enormous breakfasts that included home fries and sassy omelettes. "Can you sing on a full stomach?"

"Not if I'm sitting down."

At the jam session in his new recording studio, I didn't just listen to Andre (who was sitting down) but watched him closely. His head tips forward while playing, his beret almost covers his face as he looks at his guitar and leans into it. After all these years, his face looks pleased by the sounds that come out. The mouth harp and other guitar blend in like heart beats. I try to define the look on Andre's face as he looks down at his guitar. Respect, awe? At music school in the seventies, he was told that his guitar wasn't important, he replied "wrong answer" and quit. Besides, he already knew how to sing (palate soft, tones high) and says he didn't get whatever it was they were trying to teach him. I watch him sing. He gives his attention to the song and leans into it. It's as if his guitar speaks to him, and he sings back, and they are both in this together. Instrument and voice, voice as instrument, heart beat, soul, no drama or sentimentality or extra breath involved, plenty of humor between sets. Andre makes his songs belong.

Looking at Things Differently

If you've read this far, you're on your way to making the leap I talked about earlier. Opening up to something new prepares us to make that leap.

When I moved from the country to a small town, I began to notice yards. Living on a ranch, I was accustomed to backdrops of mountains, stands of timber, tall grass, the ebb and flow of a creek. I saw things in terms of vistas. A house with a yard opened up a different world. Accustomed to forests, I observed the few trees in my yard with wonder—apple on one side, elm on the other, Russian olive in the back and a wide spruce in the front. My yard had to be the loveliest one in town. Walking and riding my bike up and down the streets, I marveled at what I had failed to observe during previous treks, before I had my own yard. This is not a town of uniform lawns and hedges, that much I knew, but the beauty and diversity astounded me. Yards of all types, large and small, messy and neat, graced by wildflowers and willow trees, tubs of plump pansies, homemade windmills and old cars and boats (one featured a manikin dressed for fishing). A gray-haired woman had over a hundred potted geraniums in her front yard, hanging in tiers from a front fence, grouped on tree stumps, another woman of limited means had carved an English garden out of a weed patch with nothing but a wheelbarrow, flower transplants from friends, free rock and sweat.

How did I get this far along in life without paying close attention to yards? The same thing can happen when we add a baby to our lives, or a kitten. All of a sudden there are babies

...everyone on this planet is here with some special gift, whether it's sculpting or accounting. It doesn't have to be obviously creative. We're all blessed with something. I believe if we are to be happy, whole people, it's our responsibility to ourselves, each other and our creator to find out that which we have been blessed with and pursue it.
Guitarist Michael Gulezian

Singing is one of the few things where we do have control, but not in the way we think. It is control related to energy—kinetic energy and energy in motion, that's what singing is.
Bonnie Jean Triplett

11

and kittens everywhere, and all marvelous. It happens when we find love. It happens when we open up to the idea of doing something new.

There's new light in the window of your soul, there's a song in the air.

Singing as Self Discovery

I was out walking yesterday and a man's voice hollered "hey stuck up!" My near-sightedness didn't allow me to make out the person but I knew the voice. Why do we recognize voices? Bing Crosby? Barbra Streisand? Why do advertisers use Robert Mitchum for beef commercials? Lauran Bacall's voice for ship cruises? James Earl Jones for Darth Vadar in the Starwar trilogy?

"I knew that was you on the phone."

The voice is unique to the individual. We cannot get lost in the crowd because our own voice has self identity. In a world of mechanization, the voice allows us to find ourselves. We are not somebody else. We are individuals.

Learning to sing gives us a chance to explore our own uniqueness. It's more than just "I sing", satisfaction comes in on a deep level, from the necessity to feel unique.

It seems as if we are living in a time of hopeless conformity. There have been worse times but these days we know more because of the media. It's easy to lose hope in light of the bad news dished up every night on the news. Think how worrisome it would have been to watch a famine or a great plague from the Middle Ages live on TV.

We are easily duped by what we see on television and hear from our politicians. A creative person is one who does not always act on accepted beliefs.

We're all as unique as our voices. My ideas appear in my head as finished products (no work required). I have what a friend called a "fertile brain." A lot of my ideas have spun off into the universe, but so what? Creative chaos is part of my nature. The modern idea of perfection inherent in many self-help books requires that we change who we are. Even the books on dying hold the promise that if-you-change-you-will-live. This is baloney. Being human is learning to accept and even use our own failings and glories instead of rejecting who we are.

Choice is part of it. Reading about the lives of artists, especially women artists, shows us that tough choices are made while choosing the creative over more ordinary pursuits. It's a choice that is available to all of us, no matter our age. As a matter of fact, the older we get the easier it becomes to shed the "shoulds" and "have-tos' and allow our inner voices to speak. (Look for more on personal choices in chapter four: Your Turn.)

Art of any kind requires nerve, the courage to do it. Discipline plays a greater part than talent. My own life as an artist is an example. As a child, I was praised both by teachers and parents for my ability to draw. I kept this ability (my nearsightedness and refusal to wear glasses might have played a part since I saw things in shapes rather than in detail) and took up ceramic sculpture in college. Sculpting came as easily to me as drawing. I gave it up and picked up interviewing, reporting and photography when a job as a newspaper correspondent came along. By this time I had a houseful of kids, and the skills of being a reporter went hand in hand with juggling a busy life. It wasn't until I began to write fiction that I had to discipline myself to do it, do it, do it. Out of this hard work I gained a sense of myself as an artist.

We learn by doing. My cello-playing partner Lee Zimmerman says university music students who played without working at it often gave up, while the less gifted persevered and went on to playing cello for life. Keep this in mind and don't skip the walking warm-ups at the end of this section.

WHERE THE RIO GRANDE IS FLOWING
AND THE STARRY SKIES ARE BRIGHT,
SHE WALKS ALONG THE RIVER
IN THE QUIET SUMMER LIGHT...
(From "The Yellow Rose of Texas")

The "Yellow Rose of Texas" is based upon a mulatto prostitute. Before the Battle of San Jacinto in 1836, Mexican General Santa Anna had invited her to his tent instead of organizing defenses. Sam Houston and his Texans attacked, and as a result, Texas won its independence from Mexico. Although "Texas, Our Texas" is the state song, the Yellow Rose song is sometimes sung at sporting events even to this day.
Cartoonist Jim Erickson

Meanwhile, Take a Breath

I remember little about my sixth grade music teacher except her thick red lipstick, her fervor and the fact that she taught me how to breathe. When she announced during class that we should put our hands on our bellies and take in a deep breath, most of us made faces and groaned. We all knew how to breathe, and I'm certain we did breathe correctly while climbing trees or running footraces, but when confronted with sitting and doing it, we soon found we were doing it wrong: we tucked in as we breathed in and relaxed the belly on the out breath. After school that day, I taught my mother and the neighbors how to breathe properly and I still admonish friends to breathe.

When you breathe in, your belly should fill up like a balloon. Proper use of breath while singing will be taught throughout the book, but for now, try this: Sit comfortably and take in an easy deep breath. It's the same as filling up a pitcher, the bottom of the pitcher (the belly) is filled up first and the rest of the pitcher (lower and upper lungs) fills up naturally. It's called belly breathing and shouldn't be forced. Hold the full breath for a moment or two before slowing pouring it out.

Warm Ups for Singing

Early opera star Marcelina Sembrich had a clear, open voice and could perform vocal acrobatics with no sign of strain. She never faltered. Her secret? She walked several miles a day to practice breathing and spent vacations climbing mountains in Switzerland.

We warm up in order to relax and get the breath into the belly. Walking works best. Keep shoulders relaxed, neck long. Do not allow yourself to breathe through the mouth. Talk to your body and tell the tense parts to soften (certain words play tricks, "relax" can seem like a command and make the body

14

more tense). We usually hold tension in our necks, shoulders, jaw and belly, all places that need to soften up in order to sing.

Walk everyday. Walk tall and keep your ribs up. Good posture helps singing (note sidebar on Judy Collins). Keep the breath in the belly. Don't try to control anything, including your thoughts. Say hello to thoughts, being aware that the breath will encourage the negative ones to leave. On bad days, I might walk two miles (or more) before troublesome thoughts take flight.

Be gentle on yourself. The breath is natural and will respond when given time. Even if you're walking with a friend (I prefer to walk alone) keep returning to the soft belly. Feel the breath as it makes the journey from the nose to the belly, filling up the torso like water poured into a pitcher—from the bottom to the top. When you pour out the pitcher, the top leaves first. Practice this.

When you get the movement, water (breath) filling up from the bottom, release it from the top with a "haaa" sound.

Experiment with the breath as you walk. Pant like a dog. Move with the breath like a panther. Feel the breath go down into your feet. Stop walking and become a tree when you come to a secluded spot. Pretend a string is connecting the top of your head with the sky in order to get into a tree stance.

This is all natural. Don't make walking and breathing difficult.

Anything practiced for forty days becomes a habit (to keep something up that long is more difficult than it sounds). I do morning warmups that require five minutes of my time—breathing in vigorously, breathing out with a "ha." Keep in mind that the word "exercise" is another one that can make the body cringe. If working out is tedious, our bodies will do it for awhile and quit. A daily walk is better than a weekly killer.

If students agree to it, we sing outside. I live close enough to the river so we can walk there and sing. Try singing outside. When you walk and sing, you have to breathe. I hope to become known as the walking singing teacher.
Nicki Pisano

I think one of the most important things about Judy Collins was her posture. She stood straight with her head back, and she could really belt. People would just drop their teeth, they'd never seen anything like that before.
Dave Van Ronk,
sixties folks singer who
blended blues, jazz and rock

15

If you're in a wheelchair or, like me, are occasionally put down by an old knee injury, you can still practice the most essential part of singing—breathing into the belly. The other part of the body that needs familiarity in order for you to sing well is the jaw.

Why?

Because our bodies are smart and know everything. It takes work to support the tones and during a difficult piece or while singing at the upper part of a range, the body will stop depending on the breath and look for a way out. "You take over, I need a break."

What does the body turn to? The jaw, the neck, the throat and the tongue, most often the jaw since it is so powerful and ready for action. The joint that hinges our jaws (the mandibular, it even sounds important) is the strongest joint in our bodies. Think of the overall evolution, the way we had to learn to chew and get our food down, how much stress was (and still is) involved in the jaw. Many people carry stress in the jaw. My teacher worked for years getting her jaw to relax.

What adjustments are needed to make it right?

Relax your jaw and center your breath deep in the belly. It always gets back to the belly. Let the jaw hang open. Go to the library and check out a tape on learning to yodel. The exercise in my yodeling tape calls for a "stupid face"— jaw slack, tongue resting on lower lip. Try it. My high school debate coach used an ape exercise to get us to relax our jaws. Stand up, place feet wide apart and slump slightly forward from the waist, shoulders and arms relaxed (don't think too much about the stance, it comes natural). Swing the jaw from side to side while breathing from the mouth. Make a "buuu" sound. The rattling jaw will transform it into an ape-like ripple.

Yoga combines breath with stretching and is good for our bodies, our hearts and our singing. Try it. Classes are offered in a variety of places—yoga centers, health clubs, Y's, senior centers—or buy a book or video on the subject. For more musical warmups, (la, la, la, up and down the scale) turn to Part Two on voice technique.

Chapter Two
Books and Learning

Matt Olason and schoolchildren from Sanders County during a Young Author's Conference at the Hot Springs Elementary School, 1995.

Photo by Jo Rainbolt

Lamperti and the Golden Age of Music

In the small town (population 500) where I live on the Salish-Kootenai Indian Reservation in western Montana there happens to be a voice teacher with classical training who teaches a method from the 1800's (the Old Italian School of Music) in which singing is considered as natural and easy as breathing.

In fact, the founder of the method, Giovanni Battista Lamperti, summed it up by saying "The breath is the ocean, the voice the boat that floats on the ocean," and what could be more natural than that?

Lamperti's method is simple and it works, but, as with many lessons from the past, it has been almost lost. My teacher learned it from Robert Knowles, an Italian-born voice coach now living in California. When I expressed interest in Lamperti, she gave me a short biography and several pages of published notes describing the method. During my next lesson, she looked up from her piano during warmups and said, "You have balanced the breath and the tone, every note was perfectly placed."

Balancing the breath and the tone allows the boat to effortlessly skim along the ocean, it requires skills that will be discussed throughout the book. I had been practicing those skills but my tendency was to start with too much gusto, this was the first time I took off and sailed.

"That's a big leap forward. What did you do since your last lesson?"

I replied that I had read Lamperti's notes, and they made sense.

She became excited. For the first time in twenty years, she had a student who had learned by reading.

"This is the most important thing I've heard," she said, "In my experience, nowhere on the college level do they even attempt the thought that you can read about it and do it."

19

We had already decided to collaborate on a book on how to sing, the fact that it could be taught without the use of discs or tapes or a college laboratory gave us the boost we needed. Learning to sing with Lamperti is learning to breathe, it is aerobic, you will start slowly and build up to a complete workout. Since there is no strain in the throat or mouth, singing in this style is something we can do all of our lives. When asked if she had revised Lamperti's method to fit modern students' needs, my teacher paused to think for a moment and replied, "Why change it? Singing back then was the best level the human voice ever reached."

Lamperti frees us of the misconception that singing is precious, reserved for the few. There is discipline in his method but it comes from within. Children, nuns, monks, Blacks and others born into singing societies such as the Maori and our own Ozark mountain people do it naturally. If the desire is there, anyone can learn it. In my teacher's words, imagination (not talent) is what carries one forward. All of her beginning students are over forty, one woman started lessons in her mid-sixties.

Lamperti suggested that students take a year to practice nothing but breathing into the belly and singing "la" up and down the scale. It's unlikely that modern readers will slow down that much (better to take it easy and let go of expectations while teaching ourselves to sing) and, from the facts of his life, it appears that Lamperti would have had a hard time following his own advice.

Born in Milan, Italy in 1839 during the Golden Age of Singing when opera singers were as popular as sports heroes are today, Lamperti began to study piano at age six and three years later was the first soprano in the Milan Cathedral (and paid well for it). He entered the Royal Conservatory of Music in Milan at eleven and, after graduating at fourteen, began to coach Italian and German opera singers. He wrote his first musical composition "Twelve Solfeggi" at sixteen, tutored actors in singing, had a passion for flowers and, while coaching the opera greats of the day, still accompanied his father's more ordinary singing students on a daily basis.

He had been forced to take up music as a young child by his father, a voice teacher, since none of the older five siblings showed a talent for it. Lamperti was lauded as the greatest coach during a time of excellence, but he harbored a secret desire to become an actor and during his mid-life years broke with his father over the old man's incessant demands and established a music school in Dresden, Germany.

All these facts and more (the list of opera greats he coached fills two pages) were transcribed word for word by William Earl Brown, a voice student of Lamperti's in Dresden during a period of two years (1891-1893).

Singing is easy and rewarding. I hope that much has been made clear so far. Getting to the heart of it is the problem. Lamperti called it the truth. This truth, according to the words transcribed to the student mentioned above, descended by word of mouth among singers, and was not a method, but a reaction involving our mental, physical and emotional selves. It is a teachable skill.

Lamperti will be our guide in getting back the gift of song. There will be other helpers along the way.

Books as Tools

An 86-year-old Icelandic Norwegian attended a Young Author's Conference at our local school featuring an oldtime theme. Matt Olason had made his mountain man outfit from deer and coyote skins the old, hands-on way—tanned the hides with homemade tools, sewed and beaded the scabbard and moccasins and fringed shirt and leggings and pouches, trapped and tanned the coyote for the headdress and fur blankets. The tools he used to make the outfit were handmade. The kids were encouraged to ask questions.

Speech and song have long been considered attributes of man but worthy of the Gods.
Donald Proctor, M.D. from Breathing, Speech, and Song

What an exciting time it must have been when man first began to sense and employ the beauty of words to enhance the interest of the story. Perhaps the use of rhyme and rhythm increased the ability of the listener to remember and be able, in turn, to pass on the tale. It seems probable that melody and song must have been introduced at the same time. It is hard to imagine man, possessed of the ability to speak, to tell stories and to put them into poetry, without indulging in song if only as a means of celebrating those capacities.
Donald Proctor, M.D.

"Did you learn how to make your outfit from the Indians?"

"Nope. They don't do it anymore."

"Where'd you learn?"

"From books. You can learn anything you want from books."

An 83-year-old Hidatsa Indian raised in the old ways by her grandmother looked closely at the beadwork. The mountain man had paid such attention to the details in the books he read that she was able to identify which tribe the various beading styles came from.

Books on Singing

I started my writing career in a twofold way, as a journalist and a recorder of Native American folktales, both of which involved getting information firsthand from living subjects. While researching a topic, I still prefer to call on firsthand experience (my own or others), but after the mountain man's comment about learning from books, I visited the library at the University of Montana where, to my surprise, I found dozens and dozens of books on the technique involved in singing—especially the use of the breath. Written for the most part before 1920 and after 1970, some dated back to the early and mid 1800's and featured the Old Italian School from the 17th century (which, I repeat, I am learning in Hot Springs, Montana) and I was thrilled to come across "The Art of Singing" by William Shakespeare. The bard and I share the same birthday, April 23rd and, thanks to Garrison Keillor who announces famous birthday information each day on public radio, I know a few things about him. A successful businessman, Shakespeare owned half interest in a theater, encouraged writers and singers and actors, acted himself, published hundreds of sonnets and as many plays, so why not a book on singing? The book looked old enough, cardboard cover, old fashioned print, but the revised signed- by-the-author preface was dated February 18, 1921. Not the Shakespeare I was looking for, but the book had a good feel to it and the subtitle addressed a worthy topic: "Based on the Principles of the Old Italian Singing-Masters, and Dealing with Breath-Control and Production of the Voice. Together with Exercises." Skimming through it, I found quotations by Lamperti, exercises featuring ah and la and advice for perfecting breath and getting consonants right.

The books I came across are listed in the bibliography at the back of this book. Not all are readily available but can be found with a little luck and a computer (should we stop here and thank computers for bringing obscure titles into the hands of smalltowners?) I encourage you to do your own search. Even small libraries are on interloan programs, and librarians seem to feel it is their job to be helpful.

My father was in construction; we moved every few years when I was a child and, upon arrival to a new town, I got myself a library card. I recall imposing librarians who could silence a room with a glance, but I have yet to meet an impatient librarian. Perhaps it is the company they keep: the company of books.

Wandering through the stacks at the University of Montana, I picked out a book with an eye-catching cover: a precise and beautifully detailed drawing of a man's head and upper torso, larynx and breathing apparatus exposed.

"Breathing, Speech, and Song," published in Austria in 1980 by Donald Proctor, M.D., is a scientific treatise based on sound voice wisdom. Proctor, a professor of otolaryngology at John Hopkins Schools of Medicine, is a practicing laryngologist who studied voice, performed publicly as a young man and overcame his habit of stammering by speaking to medical students on, among other subjects, the physiology of singing. The message of the book to a lay reader is the same as that given to us by the Italians—understand the dynamic source of breathing, use it wisely.

"Optimum performance in speech and song results from delicate control of the breathing and vocal mechanisms," Proctor wrote, "Not from the expenditure of great force."

In other words, trust the ocean of breath and float on it. A voice does not have to wear out, even in old age.

I learned some musical history from Proctor. Speech and song have been with us in one form or another since the beginning of our time on earth. The importance of these arts to the Greeks can be noted by the attributes of the nine Greek muses: Calliope (epic poetry and eloquence), Euterpe (music and lyric poetry), Erato (love poetry), Polyhymnia (oratory and scared poetry, note the word hymn), Clio (history), Melpomeme (tragedy), Thalia (comedy), Terpsichore (choral song and dance), and Urania (astronomy). They even had a god of music in Apollo.

The genuine beauty of singing consists in a perfect union, an amalgam, a mysterious alloy of the singing and speaking voice, or, to put it better, the melody and spoken word.

Reynaldo Hahn

The character of speech and song has been with us forever, but knowledge of phonation is relatively recent, marked by the first Italian operas in 1600 ("Euridice" by Jacopo Peri and "Orfeo" by Monteverdi). A scientific document "The Larynx Organ of Voice", published the following year by a man named Casserius, is still regarded among scientists as a classic regarding the organs of breathing and the larynx. (The drawing that caught my eye on the cover of Proctor's book dated from 1601 and was done by Casserius.) Construction of the first opera house was completed in Venice in 1637 and the Golden Age of Voice was upon us.

Things got interesting. Castrating young males for soprano perfection dated back to the middle ages when the admonishment in the Bible "Let your women keep silence in church" was taken seriously. According to the laryngologist Proctor, the castrato, as the eunuch was called, had the breathing mechanism of an adult and the larnyx of the child and so possessed an unusual vocal mechanism. Proctor went on to say that, since castratos achieved unusual height, their breathing capacity exceeded ordinary adults and, coupled with the low airflow from the childlike larnyx, they could sustain long passages on a single breath. Carlo Broschi, a castrato who sang under the stage name of Farinelli, was said to have been able to hold high C for a full two minutes. The practice of castration went on for a long time. Moreschi, the last of the castrato singers, died in 1922. Books have been written about the castrato. The well-known English diarist and Naval official Samuel Pepys described their singing in his diary, claiming that he preferred "the joys of listening to their performances (to female sopranos).. Women fell in love with them, the question of marriage even came into it.." Pepys, by the way, attended fourteen operas in London in the year 1661 and became so enthusiastic about opera that he later turned to composing.

Classical music and opera corresponded with what scholars call the Age of Reason. I can't help but wonder— was this when we started to forget what we knew instinctively and had to reason it all out? Not that I have an axe to grind; even though I wasn't exposed to anything classical while growing up, I traded in a bus ticket to buy a recording of *Carmen* while traveling as a teenager and hitched a ride home. Opera moves me (more on that later) but, still, my most thrilling musical moments have been the unexpected ones involving ordinary people—the bus driver who sang all night on a dusty ride through northern Mexico and, more poignantly, the thin sweet voice of a refugee from the mountains of Laos who laughed bravely whenever the subject of leaving her homeland during the Vietnam War came up, and one day was able to sing it. I couldn't understand the words, but the feeling has never left me. That hardy mountain woman who lost her husband and sons to an unwanted war and left the homeland of her parents and grandparents sang about it, and took me with her.

More on Books

Singers, especially teachers of voice, seem to have a great desire to share their expertise. Trouble is, good singing speaks for itself. I had to sit in a straightbacked chair to get through many of these books or I found myself asleep on the sofa. Singing is not easy to write about (or do singers and voice teachers resist editors?) Still, each book contained gems of advice and my ultimate conclusion was that people in love with their subject make good company even if their prose lulls me to sleep.

Continuing my wandering through the stacks at the University of Montana, I picked up another winner: a lavender-covered book with gold letters "On Singers and Singing," nine lectures from 1913-14 by a French composer Reynaldo Hahn. Born in Venezuela in 1874 to a Venezuelan-Catholic mother and a German-Jewish father, the youngest of twelve children, Hahn moved with his family to France at age three, began singing soprano at six, and entered the Paris Conservatoire at eleven where his fluency in composition became evident. The introduction to the book (published originally as "Du Chant" and translated from the French in 1990) quotes a classmate who recalled that if the professor in composition class needed a manuscript for study he would say "Reynaldo, write something for us," and the boy would place himself before the blank page and ten minutes later, class would begin.

He sang all the time, including during his lectures, but made it clear at the beginning of the series (in a lecture entitled "Why Do We Sing?) that he didn't consider himself an expert. In other words, his ego wasn't involved in the act of singing. He wasn't afraid to discuss love of singing, and he lauded the beauty and authenticity of folk singing.

Hahn had nothing against the Old Italian method of singing. "A beautiful voice controlled by will of the singer, whether naturally beautiful or made so by training, is a most beautiful thing," he said during one of his lectures, but went on to add,

English is an extraordinary, imaginative and musical mixture of sounds.

From the musical
"My Fair Lady"

"However, a beautiful voice does not suffice; it may produce a pleasant sensation, but this has nothing to do with the real beauty of singing."

A linguist by nature, Hahn was fluent as a child in the Spanish language of his mother, the German of his father and the French of his adopted homeland. He never got over his love affair with the spoken word. Singing—putting words to music—came as natural to him as breathing.

An artistic genius living in a time and place where art was foremost, he had an appealing personality marked by humor and a lack of conceit. His spoken word reads like the best writing, yet he was more than willing to admit that he didn't know much, and that what he did know was likely to change.

"I am not a singer, not a teacher of singing...I am a composer and have only relative authority to speak on an art so complex, so arduous, that even the specialists are often contradictory."

His discourses take the complexity and hard work out of the subject of singing. He claimed to rely on instinct—sang from time to time to illustrate a point—and presented the subject of song in a hands-on style.

One of his biographers, Bernard Gavoty, described his voice as "nothing exceptional, a fine baritone, not very large, flexible as grass, ruled with a marvelous intelligence, a reflective divination. An interminable cigarette dangled from the line of his lips, not as a "pose" but out of habit. He sang as we breathe, out of necessity."

A cigarette? By the time I came across Hahn, I had immersed myself on books on singing; whether worthwhile or pedantic, all contained definite ideas concerning technique, especially posture and facial position. (Some went so far as to make it seem that singing was impossible without taking on the appearance of the hull on a battleship.) Here was a man who sang all the time while smoking. He himself referred to the habit

Vowels are open, no dipthongs; or trouble may come up. The tongue and mouth are relaxed. The mouth doesn't work; it just stays open. The back of the throat like a big, wide-open yawn. Trusting this, and relaxing the throat, makes for full, pure vowel sounds. We are not used to hearing these highly placed, pure vowel sounds in English. German and Italian sounds are good teachers.
Bonnie Jean Triplett

in his discourse on how to enunciate while singing. He had advised his listeners that grimaces with the mouth in order to sing well are not only unnecessary but distracting, and then went on to deride his own performance. How he tried (but didn't always succeed) in correcting himself of his own singing mannerisms—knitted brows, closed left eye, head slightly back which he deemed "very bad" since it adds an affectation.

"Still, after drawing attention to the ridiculous mannerisms to which I am afflicted, I am going to pay myself a compliment. It is only fair, don't you agree? My friends are often astonished that I sing with a cigarette, which I am actually smoking, between my lips. Do not think that I boast of this ability as if it were worthy of admiration. If I sing with a cigarette in my mouth it is because, unfortunately, I am a chain smoker, and the cigarette has become part of myself. But if I can keep it in my mouth without dropping it, it is because I barely move my lips while singing, and this is the compliment I pay myself. In order to articulate clearly, it is not necessary to move the lips constantly and to inflict strange shapes upon one's mouth. First, this gives a jerky quality to the singing, but more than that, when one has many words to pronounce in a short period of time, the spectacle becomes grotesque."

The musical Frenchman traveled and conducted widely, and he is well known throughout the singing world but not in the U.S. (a proposed trip didn't take place). His book of lectures "On Singers and Singing" should remedy this and is available from the publisher listed in the bibliography. Quotations from Hahn are used throughout this book.

He serves as a reminder to not lose sight of the simple pleasure of words.

Which brings us to our next topic: English.

Singing in English

Learning to sing musically in English was my greatest challenge.

Oh, to be native Italian with the most lyrical vowels on earth linking words into one bound-together phrase. It's so much easier to sing in Italian than English. Legato, an Italian word, translates "bound together," and a song in Italian flows along effortlessly. The only ones who seem to get it right with American English are black singers. They don't need to pretend to be Italians or Irish, and they don't cheat, either, by singing only the vowels and leaving out those nasty English consonants.

"I SING IN ENGLISH, BUT FOR THE REST I'LL WHISTLE IN SPANISH."

During a typical lesson, my voice teacher takes me through warmups consisting of open vowel sounds up and down the scale. At least one exercise begins with nee or nnnoe to get the placement right, but aside from the nnnn, the warmups are all open vowel sounds. I easily move to the Italian warmup songs and into the more difficult art songs in Italian and German. My placement is high; I'm not an American born in Iowa but Scottish or Irish. Then we move into English and I get scared. Those pesky English vowels and ornery consonants refuse to flow.

How to sing in English? My only recourse was to continue singing and treat English as if it were Italian. But I'd hear Ella Fitzgerald on the radio and she'd get it right. Singers like Patsy Cline sing as if they are sitting next to you at the bar and telling you a true story from their own lives. Joan Baez is another example. The genius of these singers is that they sing effortlessly. They sing legato but it's in English, and their words tell a story.

English is my language. I love the nuances of expression, the endless juxtaposition of subjects and nouns, the playful and hard working verbs. I write in English, I'm not afraid to speak it in front of strangers in a voice recognizably my own, so why can't I sing in it?

The people sing and make music to re-establish the good and beautiful in the world.
  Ethnologist Tony Seeger from his book *"Why Suya Sing"*

When we stop singing, we will really be finished.
  from the book *"Why Suya Sing"*

I think of my friend Andre who warms up by talking over an omelette and hashbrowns. Consonants don't bother him. Still, most singers of English have my problem. We might be able to talk clearly but we eat the language while singing. Did you ever hear an opera sung in English? The screeching and harshness makes one long for Italian. The same thing happens to pop singers. The same thing happens to me.

What if this isn't a problem of language but of our rendition of it? What if the vowels we grew up with can serve us very well, and even those pesky English consonants play a major role in a song?

All this and more has been convincingly presented in "To Sing in English: A Guide to Improved Diction" by Dorothy Uris, a book written in 1971 (see bibliography for more details). Uris, a speech therapist and consultant, was issued an invitation by singer and voice teacher Lotte Leonard to sit and listen to well-trained voices singing what Uris called "a puzzling mixture of mannerisms and localisms." These Americans were professional singers who could sing the notes, but not convey the message of the song in English.

"What's going on?" Uris asked, to which Madame Leonard replied, "You tell me."

Why do English speakers murder English songs? Uris found the subject so challenging she stayed with it, researching, proselytizing and teaching speech and diction at schools of music, coaching for opera companies (including the Metropolitan and Santa Fe) and writing a book about it.

The book is written with professional singers in mind, she assumes we all know how to lean on the breath and maintain a musical line, but there are lessons in it for all of us. Think of it as learning a new way to put together foods for optimum health, taste and nutrition (not to mention color and esthetics). We can do this with the ingredients already familiar to us: nouns and verbs.

We have a fear of grammatical rules in this country that stands right up there with our phobia of speaking in public. The simple words: noun, verb, adjective, adverb are enough to instill dread. Who should take the blame for this? The old-fashioned teachers of grammar that some of us encountered in grade school? The later teachers who did not teach by the old rules? Relax. What we need to sing well in English might sound like a lesson in grammar, presented as punishment for being bad and sloppy, but is simply a method for learning the built-in beat of English. Trust me, this beat is not difficult to learn and is being taught for a reason. It is worth your time to not skip this chapter.

Built-in Inflection

Without knowing how words work, we cannot sing well in any language. There is a built-in inflection to English speech that is honored during ordinary activities such as reading aloud (reading to kids is great training ground) or making conversation, but not while singing. It helps to pay attention to the naturalness of speech inflection. For instance, this morning I went for a short walk (a common occurrence while writing) and looked up to see a stranger directly across the street, a heavy set scruffy fellow in a brown leather jacket about to light up a cigarette. We happened to notice each other at the same moment and rather than look the other way, I asked "How are you?" And he cheerfully replied "fine." As I walked on, I analyzed the brief exchange according to what I had just been reading in Uris' book on diction. The tone of my inquiry was light but the fact that I had emphasized you—"How are YOU?" made it friendly. "How ARE you?" is intimate, implying concern for a man I don't even know. Actors, TV and radio commentators and others whose livelihoods rely on speech are no doubt aware of speech inflection, and it's a good thing for singers to be aware of, too.

After staying up half the night with author Uris, I go to bed exhausted. The lessons from Uris are worth learning, but repressed memories of cramming for a college exam are surfacing. Diagrams of the vowel ladders and circles of consonants swirl around in my brain. In the morning I question myself while I make tea. I am housesitting for a friend forty miles west of home in a neighborhood of deep green. The town, Thompson Falls, sits on a reservoir and reminds me of every water place I've ever loved—river towns along the Mississippi traveling to see my grandmother in Iowa, my first married year on the Pike River in northern Wisconsin (now designated a wild river, a sacred place with no humans allowed to live on its banks), raising my kids on the meandering Bitteroot River in Montana and, for a brief time, living along the Southeast Straits of Alaska. But I'm also reminded how oppressive river places can be during times of heavy rain. It's May but spring has missed Thompson Falls. Heavy clouds hang over the mountains and the rain is like a giant bird that swoops over the town even when the sun is out. This is a town of alleys and giant evergreens, cedars and jackpines—a country town but still the largest in my county (the longest county in Montana, stretching all the way to Idaho and not a traffic light in it, although espresso has arrived). We also have the greatest weather extremes in the state. Dry on one end of the county where I live and wet here. It was sunny when I left home; I'd planned to write on my friend's deck, not holed up in the kitchen with a wood fire.

But then, the morning sun comes out and, even though the mountains held dark clouds, I take my tea outside on the deck where I question my muse.

I am a novice singer, why am I writing this book? My muse is big and black, a wild woman of the north who eats smalltown gossip for breakfast and shelters the unfortunate under her ribcage. She would have no problem singing. Still, she has not helped me with this particular project.

The answer comes not from within but from the voice of a child a few blocks away. The town, wrapped in rain, is quiet as the wilderness but this child's voice brings with it the promise of summer.

I hear the words "I am" and the rest is ancient melody. This is a toddler singing his or her heart out (why did I first assume it was a boy? My oldest daughter, the one who "cannot sing" used to sing in a blessed roar and roll in the tall grass on sun-washed mornings). A few minutes later this toddler's song turned to a cry for mother but while I sat with my tea the child spoke to me, her voice-as-instrument, high, melodic, ancient, carrying clearly over the tops of green trees in a mountain town.

Why do we sing? Because our hearts are full—the same reason we do anything creative—and song can be done while our hands are filled with work or children or springtime. We sing for ourselves and out of an ancient praise.

I reminded myself to proceed gently. Do the same, dear reader. Learning to sing is, after all, a natural activity. When we relax, we become receptive as small children. Uris has something to say and I have something to learn: English is not more difficult or less pretty to sing than the accepted song languages (German, Italian and French). It is simply different.

What Makes English "Different"

English is a stress language. Every language has intrinsic features which convey meaning to the listener. In English, we have strong word-types that receive more attention (greater stress) than the weak word-types that simply link the sentence together. For this reason, linguists call it a stress language. This, by the way, should not be confused with nervous stress but is another kind of stress, an emphasis, a built-in beat that is entirely natural to the native speaker and is only noticeable if it is lacking, as it often is in song.

English is more strongly accented than other languages of the vocal repertoire (most of the world's art songs are written in Italian, German, French or English). Singers may pronounce every vowel and consonant, or project every word, and the song will not sound right.

I didn't know I was doing it , but I sing during surgery. A woman from Butte said, "Doc, I don't mind your singing, but Christmas carols in July?" And another patient said he was really nervous until he heard me singing and figured if I was that relaxed, he'd ease up.

Richard Beighle,
chief ophthalmologist at the
Rocky Mountain Eye Center,
Missoula, Montana

Uris was referring to English-speaking singers when she said, "Singers need to develop extra-sensitivity, a bodily response to the language's rhythm."

The quality that gives English its unique flavor lies in the vivid contrasts of strong and weak word-types. These unique speech rhythms of stress and unstress, natural to us as speakers, needs to be consciously grasped by singers in order to be understood. In Uris' words, "how the listener receives lyric messages from the sender (the singer)."

What Uris is urging us to do is to get back to the child's way of perceiving language. Remember how we read the message of adults even if the words were too big to understand?

"Song, a form of communication unlike any other, binds sender and receiver in a reciprocal exchange of feelings and pleasure." No matter their school or technique, the experts would be in accordance with that statement by Uris. However, she wasn't finished, but added, "from which meaningful language can never be absent."

I would qualify that last statement since beautiful songs have the power to move me whether or not I know the meaning of the language. Remember the songs of the Maori mentioned in the preface? Hearing them, I felt the oneness of breath that makes us human. Song is a universal language, the boat that floats on the ocean of breath. Still, I will concede the linguistic point to Uris and relate another example from my travels in Mexico. This time the speaker was a Mexican pilot; while giving an overview of the flight in English, he pronounced the words without the inflection we naturally give the language. It sounded like a tonal language, interesting to the ear but unintelligible to the Americans on board. Except for the rolled r's, he could have been speaking in Chinese.

It wasn't a short monologue, the man had probably studied his script and wanted to show it off. "That's English," I told my pre-teen daughter.

"It is?" She was amazed.

This brings us around to personal style: what makes your song sound like you? It is something people who have sung since childhood grasp intuitively; however, the rest of us (who can speak without hesitation) become wooden while singing. "The genius of a language is reflected in its speech sounds." Uris writes, "The vowels and consonants of English mutually enhance each other to the great advantage of song."

Is it important enough to learn?

One of the first things my voice teacher said was "singing is speaking in musical tones." She gave examples. "Listen to Patsy Cline, words come one into the other, almost a conversation." Patsy Cline did it naturally, she had it down, the inner beat of words to song. I didn't want to sound like Patsy Cline. I wanted to sound like me, but I wanted to know how she did it.

Listen carefully to the ease of delivery and lack of pomposity that makes the listener want to keep listening. Good modern singers rely on the breath in the same way as early opera singers. Since you picked up this book, chances are you love singing and have a personal collection of tapes or CDs. If a favorite tape is available, stop reading for a few minutes, stand up and stretch, and put on a song that you never get enough of. Perhaps you were already listening to music as you read. If you're traveling or away from home, make a note to yourself to resist the boob tube upon returning home and to sit down and play a favorite song instead. TV has become a habit even with music lovers.

We are Americans and therefore well armed with equipment, most of us have small tape recorders that have been replaced by CD players or entertainment centers. Dig out that tape player or borrow one from a neighborhood teenager. I have one right here in my desk drawer, a handy little model with ear phones that one of my kids gave me to listen to while walking. I never got in the habit of using it but I will now. It has a fast forward and reverse so I can listen over and over to the same song, or the same line.

Put in a tape that contains a favorite song. Listen not to the words but to the musical line. Chances are it will flow along. The beat, the tempo, the delivery, all this can be picked up later, for now we are listening for the ease that comes with proper use of breath (the singer doesn't have to know what's going on, some do it naturally). It is this ease, this natural flow that makes us want to hear a song again and again.

You are probably already singing along. Imitate the blow by blow delivery but stay with the breath. Don't push or force the breath. Ease is deceptive. It is neither loud nor soft but vital. It is quiet. It is freedom. Ease can't be taught but must be felt. It is what we lack in modern life.

Once this ease is felt, it's simply a matter of leading through strength, or selecting key words to convey our message. In English, we have the choice of four strong word-types: nouns, active verbs, adjectives and adverbs. The small words simply connect the essential ones, in telegrams or newspaper headlines, the small words are left out, in singing they are underplayed which not only saves the singer's energy but delivers the meaning of the song.

Editors become adept at scanning stories for headlines, lines in songs can similarly be scanned. Take one of my favorite Patsy Cline songs. The first line, *'Today I passed you on the street and my heart fell at your feet.'* For me, it requires a lot of energy even if I lean into my breath Lamperti-style, and I still don't have the feeling behind the words. But I applied the telegraph test suggested by Uris. *Passed You, Heart Fell.*

'I can't help it if I'm still in love with you' becomes 'Still Love You'. In my search for essentials I had to leave out 'I can't

help it' but found that gave me energy to emphasize the last strong words about still being in love. By this time I'm thinking I might be good at this even though I am an excessive person who gathers too much information, I appreciate economy and often use the information I gather in an abbreviated form.

'Somebody else stood by your side, and she looked so satisfied.'

That one's tough to break down.

What's important? Somebody else.

Repeat refrain. The nice thing about popular music is that it's easy. The tough thing is that easy takes conscious effort. The word is ease, not lazy.

I always did have a hard time with this next stanza:

'A picture from the past came slowly stealing
as I brushed your arm and walked so close to you.
Then suddenly I got that old time feeling.'

Picture Stealing,
brushed arm,
old time feeling.

The above is highly abbreviated (I am not listening to how Cline did it but merely have the words without notes in front of me) but getting this stanza down to essentials helps me sing it. After the refrain, there is one more stanza:

'It's hard to know another's lips will kiss you and hold
you close the way I used to do. Oh, heaven only
knows how much I miss you.'

Another's lips kiss, hold close. Miss you.

I can't help it if I'm still in love with you.

We learned grammar in grade (or grammar) school and I'm not going to put us through that again except to review the most important parts of speech: nouns which designate things or persons, and active verbs which set things in motion.

The thing (noun) plus the action (verb) is all that's needed to communicate. The performer should look for those two essentials in each English phrase.

I am presently learning a beautiful song by Handel that happens to be the same one Uris used to demonstrate the two essentials:

Where-e'er you walk cool gales shall fan the glade,
Trees where you sit shall crowd into a shade.

Gales fan glade,
Trees crowd shade.

To repeat, when strong word-types are properly stressed, the meaning becomes clear. The song is prettier. It is yours. Adjectives and adverbs, the other two strong word-types in English, are helpers that enhance the meaning of nouns or verbs.

Back to Patsy Cline and the telegraph/headline lesson. I instinctively picked out strongword-types without labeling them nouns and verbs. My strong suit is not grammar (I rely on instinct), so I will pick out an obvious example from the third stanza. The verb stealing is enhanced by the adverb "slowly." Walked (verb) close (adverb) is another example, although I chose to leave that out when shortening the message. It's up to us to find out what works.

A simple example from a folk song in Uris' book further clarified the matter of expression for me. Remember Joan Baez' rendition?

Black, black, black is the color of my true love's hair.

Singing the song, I would latch on to black as if it were a life preserver and, even though my breath held out (again, thanks to Lamperti) by the time I got to the hair there was no place to go. The three blacks (all adjectives despite their appearance at the head of the line) connect nicely with color and leads into hair. This might sound like so much technical gibberish or make-work, but the point is: it works.

As the writer Uris says when she goes on about "black, black.." "And what about LOVE's hair? Is love an adjective or what? The label matters not, the function does: love's modifies hair. This simple example in a folk song prepares the way for the more complex in vocal literature."

Ever wonder why Christmas hymns sound so lovely? Because most of us, regardless of religion, grew up hearing them, and we give the phrases proper inflection.

Chapter Three
Learning From the Past

Kenny Trowbridge spellbinds a St. Louis audience in 1982 with his tall tales and songs.
Photo by Jo Rainbolt

Look to Opera

I go through times when the Lamperti technique seems old fashioned and obscure. Who needs it? Who needs to practice proper posture and songs in Italian? How many potential opera singers are reading this book?

The Lamperti technique IS worth learning. It is the best there is. I didn't start singing until middle age and intend to keep it up for at least three decades. We've all heard of singers burning out. What usually burns out is the throat. The old Italian singing style teaches us to relax the throat and rely on stronger parts of the body—the gut, the heart, the head. Trust me. It works. And if you get that word opera out of your head and approach it with the openness of a child, it isn't difficult, it's fun.

Which makes me wonder: why do opera and opera singers get a bad rap? Perhaps opera is meant to be taken personally. I'd never heard it until my second marriage. My former husband was a fan, and the tapes and records he played struck me as dark, almost demonic. In those days, everything was sunny side up for me. I let him carry the darker side of life, including opera.

One winter in the '70's, I turned on the radio each time I sat down to sew (living in rural areas makes public radio as necessary as oxygen). My project that winter was not a creative one: I was sewing nylon, down-filled jackets for my kids from pre-cut kits. One Saturday morning, I failed to turn off the radio when the weekly opera came on. I don't recall which opera it was but I do recall how quickly I was caught up by the darks and lights, the highs and lows, the terrific drama. I generally sew with a casual abandon, and the precision required to make those jackets had been driving me crazy. The operatic lunacy relaxed me. I listened and sewed every Saturday morning.

I like the idea of classical music; that is, composing something that's fixed, and playing it every time. It's working on the execution; the music is already written out, so it's just the interpretation.

Mandolinist David Grisman, godfather of '70's bluegrass/ acoustic jazz sound

"THIS IS THE WRONG BUILDING, SIR! THE **HORSE OPERAS** ARE AT THE PHILISTINES' THEATER DOWN THE STREET THERE!"

41

Singers From the Past

More recently, I heard old opera tapes during a fund raiser for Montana Public Radio. Not just Enrico Caruso, but Lotte Lehmann, Luisa Tetrazzini and Rosa Ponselle. With names and voices like that, I had to hear more. "Legendary Voices" by Nimbus Records introduced me to a whole new world. (Available at book and music stores or from Nimbus.)

Faces and backgrounds of the singers were provided in the liner notes by Nigel Douglas. I'd heard Caruso, of course, hasn't everyone? Ah, but to see his photograph. How could I not love the man, with his flourishing mustache, kind eyes and ample belly? I was dismayed to see the dates behind his name (1873-1921). Such a short life for a great man. I understood the emotion behind the Italian words of the song he sang from the opera "Lo Schiavo." When I read Douglas's description of the piece: "Americo, an officer in the Lusitanian army, is in love with his father's maidservant, Ilara. He sings of his love for the girl, 'When you were born, the flowers were born, the sun was born.'"

Rosa Ponselle became real to me: same oval-shaped face and long neck as my daughter Kristen, same large, expression-filled eyes. Rosa is dark, Kristen fair. To my delight, there was a Norwegian among the opera singers: Kirsten Flagstad.

Norway's Kirsten Flagstad had the rare ability to create moods. She was forty when she made her first performance at the Metropolitan Opera House, "...she brought every shade of feeling to her singing... her rich and eloquent voice projected the most subtle emotions to her listeners, never had they heard a voice so powerful and ringing, yet so gentle and smooth. Here was a new experience." Age did not diminish her power and resonance. Fifteen years later, in her role of Isolde at the Met, the audience got so carried away she was forced to take thirty curtain calls.

In 1926, when she was 65, Ernestine Schumann-Heink sang a concert at Carnegie Hall in New York on the fiftieth anniversary

I grew up with an incredibly wide span of music. I'm a radio baby for sure. We had rhythm-and-blues, classical, pop ballads, Grand Ole Opry, Metropolitan Opera, and the church. I was a snob of a kid, 'cause there was a time if it wasn't classical I wasn't interested.

Odetta

(her unique style of folk, classical, blues and jazz has influenced many generations of performers) of her debut in the same hall as a girl of 15 in Beethoven's Ninth Symphony. A plain woman, she debunked the idea that opera stars must be beautiful. She also refused to limit herself to opera and toured with the Roxy's, a theatrical group. This shocked the purists but her popularity never diminished, a popularity based on an astonishing three octave range. She also debunked the notion that high notes were it for a female opera star. She could reach the high notes of a soprano with ease, but it was her lower range that astonished listeners. She was so popular with the American public they refused to let her retire; she appeared on the Metropolitan Opera Stage at age 71.

Like Rosa Ponselle, Kirsten Flagstad made it big overnight, although the Norwegian had sung in provincial Scandinavian opera houses for twenty years before performing at the Metropolitan Opera, and becoming the foremost Wagnerian soprano of her day. She had long heavy braids, huge deep-set eyes looking off into the distance and a tranquil but serious expression. Lotte Lehmann, on the other hand, was leaning against a wall holding a bull's horn. Her eyes, half closed, looked at the viewer, her brow was furrowed, her mouth slightly open. She was a dish. I'd loved hearing her songs on radio. In the liner notes, Douglas said she immersed herself in everything she sang, each song had a story to tell, and it didn't matter if the subject matter was a flower, or the moon. In one song (from a Schumann group entitled "Myrten"), a night-blooming lotus in love with the moon and afraid of the sun is depicted with the same passion Lotte lavished on her stage heroines.

In 1850, Jenny Lind, "the Swedish nightingale," gave her first New York concert which was attended by 7000 cheering people. Not everyone could afford tickets but that didn't matter. At midnight of her first day in the city, 30,000 admirers gathered in front of her hotel and a band of firemen in uniform serenaded her. She was paid $10,000 for her performance, which she immediately gave to charities of the city. The most modest and the best loved of all the opera greats, she continued her gifts of

43

charity throughout her life. When advised that she was probably being used, she replied, "It doesn't matter—if I help ten people and only one deserves it, I will be content."

After the death of her father when she was twelve, Marian Anderson earned money by singing in church choirs; at that age, she already sang three octaves with such power and richness it was impossible to label her "soprano" or "alto." This self-taught singer of great soul was made famous by radio. She sang hundreds of songs in nine languages from Handel's great arias to the simplest of spirituals. In 1941 she received the great-artist Bok Award, and gave the ten thousand dollars to scholarships for promising singers. One of our greatest shames as a nation happened in 1939 when the auditorium at Constitution Hall in Washington D.C. was closed to her because she was black. She sang the scheduled performance outside at the Lincoln Memorial, and sang more gloriously than ever.

The elegant Lily Pons traveled with an entourage in grand style befitting a concert artist of the 1940's. She could handle gritty reality, too, and gave fifty concerts to a half million soldiers during WWII. In Italy, she was so close to the line she could hear firing; weary troops listened gratefully to her brilliant coloratura singing, but when she noticed a soldier who had fallen asleep, she got angry and chided herself, "You must be slipping, you can't hold an audience anymore." Her next thought was that the music was having exactly the right effect, "If music is able to rest these tired men so they can relax and fall asleep easily, I'm doing what I came across the ocean to do." From then on, she counted the dozing heads, and was grateful for each additional man who dozed off.

The only British opera star during those early years was Eva Turner. She looked a little like Elizabeth Taylor with Mary Pickford's sweetheart lips and was known as an international unforgettable dame who lived until age 98. Many of the early sopranos and some of the men lived exceptionally long lives.

Luisa Tetrazzini appears the proper maiden in her photo: eyes downcast, hair marcelled in finger waves, dressed like a school marm on Sunday in a high-collar lace bodice with a tasteful pearl and diamond brooch and modest earrings. However, she was described by Nigel Douglas as the most engaging of the great old-timers. He wrote, "Short and spherical, she pumped out her dazzling bursts of coloratura with a gusty abandon that typified her whole attitude towards life." Her memoirs tell remarkable tales of falling into the hands of bandits, being loaded with diamonds by South American presidents, having young men threaten to kill themselves if she did not kiss them. She earned more money than any Italian star except Caruso and managed to die shameless and penniless.

Lily Pons (1904-1976)
French Soprano

I met Emma Calve, a larger-than-life singer from the 1890's, in a slender book I plucked off the shelf in the Missoula Public Library titled "Famous Women Singers." Young and unknown, with little formal training and no credits under her name, she wrote a letter to the director of the Brussels opera and managed to get an audition. She replied "Yes!" when asked if she could learn the lead in *Faust* in two weeks and was a hit. Born in France near the Spanish border, Calve grew up speaking both languages and became entranced by the gypsies as a child. When she wasn't running away to observe their singing and dancing, she was spending time listening to the shepherds on the family farm. Sent to a nearby convent school for education, she invented melodies and put words to the shepherds' ghost stories, keeping the other children entertained (and probably scaring them to death). The nuns encouraged her creativity. When she took up opera, she decided a great singer could also be a dramatic actress. After becoming accepted on the European operatic stage, she went to Italy to study. "In Italy, I can learn how to send my feelings across the stage, so the audience will feel the music the way I do." She studied her roles as she'd studied the gypsies and shepherds as a child, even visiting a mental hospital for her role of Ophelia in *Hamlet* and playing the part with a lost expression, aimless movements and a stumbling walk. Contrary to the tradition of woodenness in operatic performances, Calve stayed true to her own instincts. Her sense of play, lifelike actions and dramatic truth worked—throughout her career, the public and critics lauded her (see sidebar in cowboy section for an example).

A voice I kept returning to on the "Legendary Voices" CD was that of a Russian bass, Alexander Kipnis. He sang two numbers: a serene aria by Mozart and, in contrast, a deeply dramatic song by Schubert. Both were sung in German, and I played the Schubert piece over and over, simply to hear the only two words I could understand—"my father, my father!" The words carried such depth of feeling the hair stood up on the back of my neck. During a recent special in which Schubert's songs were discussed on public radio, I got to hear the meaning behind that song: A father rides horseback through the woods on a dark and stormy night, his son with him in the saddle; the little boy sees the ghostly Spirit King, cries out and is dead in his father's arms when they reach home.

The masterful Russian singer, by the way, was striking for his ordinariness: thin hairline, round Russian face, chubby nose. I've described the females from "Legendary Voices" in detail but the men are memorable, too. Jussi Bjorling—a young Swede with a heartstopping tenor shaded by a hint of Nordic melancholy—was internationally known by age 26. The jovial-looking Titi Gobbi was a showstopping singing actor. Tenor Tito Schipa stayed delicately poised on the breath (sounding flute-like) and performed for 52 years.

Today's Oldtimers

Such verve continues. An article in *SmithsonianMagazine*, "The Aria Never Ends in the Opera That's Casa Verdi" by Richard Covington describes an old folks home in Milan, Italy, built by the great 19th century composer Giuseppe Verdi for opera divas, conductors, composers and musical performers.

Recognizing that those who performed his works often died penniless, Verdi had the home built before his death in 1901.

"It's a rest home where the residents are much too busy to rest, a retirement haven where hardly anyone is retiring. The themes of great opera flourish here—love, death, passion, jealousy, betrayal, more jealousy, tragedy, tears and triumph. Verdi would be pleased," Covington wrote, "What is missing is the dreary state one normally associated with old age and nursing homes: depression. During my visits the residents were positively ebullient."

Color photos capture this ebullience. Eraldo Coda, 91-year old former basso at the renowned opera house La Scala, stands beaming with his new bride, a violinist who also lives at the home. Residents are free to come and go—the Codas had just honeymooned through Europe by car using his newly acquired driver's license. 98-year old Santuzza Cervetti was photographed at the piano where she still played Chopin from memory. Beaming and beautiful at 89, Valentina Villa showed off photos from her 20-year career as a lyric soprano.

Among the first patrons was the renowned composer Arturo Toscanini. Each spring, an opera from La Scala is held at the palacious Casa Verdi, a tradition that began with Toscanini. Patrons sometimes attend the opera and sit in the royal box. A yearly outing features twenty Milan cab drivers who line up with a police escort and take the residents to a fancy restaurant in the country. Leave it to the Italians.

Verdi, who grew up poor, made money with his music and invested it wisely. A multimillionaire by today's standards, it saddened him to see even renowned singers and composers die in poverty. He designed the home for "musicians less fortunate than I," and stipulated that they always be treated as honored guests. The Casa wasn't opened until his death because he didn't want to attract attention. Four women and five men moved in October 12, 1902. A thousand retired performers have lived in

I grew up in Greenwich Village, and it was the most wonderful experience. I moved into the Village in 1938 when I was about two. The Village then was about eighty-five percent Italian and the rest were artists, Bohemians, and counterculturists. It was a good balance. Italians have a tendency, from a cultural position, to view artists as sort of benign idiots blessed by God. Their idiosyncratic behavior was of no particular threat to them as long as the artists were in the minority.

Mary Travers of
Peter, Paul and Mary

That's what music is at its best, a force for social change and a force for good. That's why the music of the sixties is so important. It was good, it made a statement, and it did its part in moving society...all good music makes some kind of impact or statement. Lionel Richie's "Hello" makes an impact. Tina Turner's "Private Dancer" makes a statement. Good music is good music no matter what decade we're in.

Joan Baez

the three-storied Casa Verdi. Today there are 60 guests, women and men about equally divided.

Rivalries abound among these people described by Covington as "larger-than-life characters, alive with personality, strong opinions and a collective brio that mocks their age." But it's not rivalry or theatrics that keeps these exceptional people going.

As resident Fedora Baratella puts it: "It's the music. The ones who still teach, or play or sing for their own pleasure, are the ones who remain young."

Pop Music

Americans sang all the time before World War I. Sheet music was as common as today's videos. Popular songs sold millions of copies. The songs, written to be sung by everybody, had to meet three criteria: easy to sing, play and remember.

Would-be composers moved to New York because that's where the action was. Some became famous overnight. Most of their names have been forgotten but the songs live on.

When we sing at the local nursing home, we rely on the oldies but goodies. Those of us who didn't come of age during the pre-television twenties and thirties still slide easily into the songs. They are part of our national heritage, reflecting a time when all of us whistled or sang the same tune.

And the tune, if it was good enough, did not die when the next tune came along. These standards are good songs to add to your personal songbag.

A Few Composers

Stephen Foster wrote the first popular American songs. Other composers were still looking to Europe when he wrote "Old Folks at Home" in 1851. Born in Pittsburgh to a fairly well-off and loving family in 1826, his talent for music was recognized early but not encouraged since the entertainment industry at that time was considered vulgar. His parents tried to interest him in a decent occupation and sent him to Cincinnati to work as a bookkeeper for his elder brother, a steamboat agent. Young Foster spent his spare hours by the docks along the Ohio River, listening to the work songs of the blacks and watching the adventuresome take off for Oregon Territory. A self-taught piano, flute and violin player with a pleasing baritone, he sang and wrote down the songs playing in his head and, when he returned home at age 24, announced that he intended to be a composer.

(SONG POPULAR AROUND 1860)

"OH, WHERE IS MY WANDERING BOY TONIGHT-
THE JOY OF HIS MOTHER'S PRIDE ?
HE'S TREADING THE TRACK WITH HIS BED
ON HIS BACK,
OR ELSE HE IS BUMMING A RIDE."

Singing minstrels who caricatured black life (usually white singer/comedians with "burned cork" faces) were America's favorite entertainers, and Foster happily wrote songs for the minstrel shows. More serious musicians looked down on such earthiness, and for a time he followed their lead and began to write "Ethiopian melodies" under an assumed name. But when his simple "Old Folks at Home" became a huge hit, he decided to follow his heart and write songs that entertained and stirred the emotions of ordinary people. He continued to write songs for the people and left a legacy of enduring favorites. The trade of tunesmith gained respect because of Foster, but his pleasure-loving, easygoing ways, got him into trouble financially; he never could manage his substantial royalties and died in poverty at age 37.

It's sometimes assumed that Foster wrote "Carry Me Back to Old Virginny," the official anthem of that state, but that song and "In the Evening by the Moonlight" were both written by a black composer, James Bland, before the age of twenty.

Born in New York in 1854, his educated and cultured family was similar to Foster's in that they wanted their son to choose a respectable career. However, music prevailed. While a student at Howard University, he even organized a black minstrel show, much to the horror of college authorities who regarded theater,

I had no illusions about a career in music..my reason for working was, frankly, to pay the bills. I love to sing. I was totally devoted to my work.. other college wives worked in the library or as secretaries..my job was to go to these places and sing. After the initial intimidation I found New York to be my natural home. A sort of zeal came over me and I saw there was something I had to communicate. I didn't think of myself as a singer as much as a storyteller anyway.

Judy Collins

49

Blues will never die. It goes on and on like 'old man river.' It always stays in the spotlight. There are so many fans. This rock and roll punk stuff, it comes and goes. But blues never goes. Some of the rock and roll comes from the blues.
John Lee Hooker

I don't even remember if we had a radio when I was a kid in Missouri. Enjoyment was going from home to home, getting together around the piano and singing the pop songs of the teens and twenties. My family moved to Montana in 1934 and, after I married Hugh, we sang at weddings and funerals. He had seven brothers who liked to gather around the piano. Times have changed; everything is faster.
Virginia Butler

and especially minstrel, as the work of the devil. His desire was to work with a minstrel group but, ironically, his black face didn't fit in with the whites burnt cork faces. When he did find an all- black group, he wrote hundreds of popular tunes on the road. The group went abroad and became a sensation in London, playing at Buckingham Palace and wowing crowds all over the country. When the group returned to the states, Bland stayed overseas for twenty years. He was the highest paid performer of his day but, like Foster, died in poverty.

The five Von Tilzer brothers fared better. Born in Indianapolis in the 1870's, they all followed the lead of Harry, the eldest, and became successful in the popular music industry. Harry left home at age 14 in a boxcar to join the circus and a traveling repertory theater. By the time he arrived in New York at 20, he'd written songs, replaced the family name of Gumm with Von Tilzer, and was an old hand at vaudeville and burlesque. Within ten years, he had his own publishing firm and was making a fortune from songs he'd written ("A Bird in A Gilded Cage," "On a Sunday Afternoon," "My Old New Hampshire" and many others). He became known as the number one man in Tin Pan Alley and is credited with inspiring the name for the center of the publishing business. (A reporter heard him trying out a new song on his tinny piano and named it Tin Pan Alley.) All the brothers had musical ability but three stayed in the business end of song writing. Albert, self taught like the others, studied harmony and classical voice when he came to New York, and became the best musician of the lot.

When he published a hit song, "Teasers," he followed a man for two blocks to hear him whistle it on the streets. It was Albert who came up with the classic "Take Me Out to the Ballgame."

Unlike the Von Tilzers, most composers wrote only the music while lyricists wrote the words. Few composers became publishers, a risky business, and fewer sang their own songs.

Yet one of the few successful female songwriters, Carrie Jacobs-Bonds, did it all—wrote music and lyrics, published (in her bedroom) and plugged her work.

Born in Janesville, Wisconsin, in 1862 into a well-off and happy family, she was left penniless with a nine-year-old son to raise after a series of tragedies that included her father and husband's early deaths. Determined to make it on her own, she moved to New York and rented what was called a "hall bedroom." After a year of grief when music seemed to have left her, she again took up song writing, not happy songs this time, but simple and heartrending songs that reflected her own experience with loss. She couldn't get them published so borrowed money from a friend, found a printer, and, with the help of her young son, started The Bond Shop in the one-room apartment. She couldn't afford a decorated cover so painted them herself with wreaths of wild roses. "As Unpretentious As a Wild Rose" became her slogan and the classic "I Love You Truly" her first song. More followed, her son quit school and delivered them to music stores on his bicycle, but the songs weren't pushed and didn't sell. No longer young, she took the plunge and performed at private parties and public performances. Described as "tall and regal" with a rich contralto voice, she played piano and preferred to recite rather than sing her songs. Once she was hissed from the gallery at a Chicago vaudeville house, but she never gave up. A break came when Jessie Bartlett Davis, prima donna of the Boston Opera Company, performed her songs. As other singers followed, the nation began to buy her sheet music. Her biggest success was "A Perfect Day," inspired by an outdoor outing with friends and the pleasure of their company. It sold millions of copies. She was a brave and modest woman, loved by friends. In her epitaph, Herbert Hoover wrote that her songs "express the loves and longings, sadness and gladness of all people everywhere...truly folk music of the world."

Southern Negroes sang about everything. Trains, steamboats, steam whistles, sledge hammers, fast women, mean bosses, stubborn mules—all become subjects for their songs. They accompany themselves on anything from which they can extract a musical sound or rhythmical effect, anything from a harmonica to a washboard. In this way, and from these materials, they set the mood for what we now call the blues.

William Handy from his autobiography

Some of them (younger singers) are pretty good, but they still don't have the time and feeling that we had. They have different things on their minds. We'd think about the times, you know (the thirties) and all that was against us.

Honeyboy Edwards, still performing the Delta blues at 81

51

Our Holy Roller neighbor would come down and pound on the piano and when one of us kids made a snide remark about it, Dad—who got away from his church when he left home and seldom said much—smiled and said, "I kind of enjoy it. The only thing I miss is the singing. They had so much fun."

Liz Fee

A blues song lets you put yourself in the place of someone else. You listen and say, 'I know how that guy feels.' 'How would I feel if that happened to me?' When you're in a position to put things in a poetic form, it creates sweetness, understanding and emphasis. Some people just get up and recite a poem. I think when you sing it in a blues form you get more attention for it.

Willie Dixon,
blues singer and bass player

Things Get More Professional

Around the time of WWI, dancing swept the nation, and it wasn't enough for a song to be sung and remembered; it had to have a good dance rhythm, and be sung and played by pros. Silent movies came in and theme songs replaced simpler melodies. The automobile took Americans out of their living rooms and into the theaters and dance halls. Pianos (every middle-class home had one) became pieces of furniture.

After the war, the recording industry boomed as player pianos and phonograph companies made recordings of the latest hits. Sheet music dropped drastically in sales.

Change happens. Americans weren't singing as much, but they still had music in their homes through records, and they were dancing. And one of the sweet, surprising things that came out of this era of productivity and professionalism was the birth of the blues.

Father of the Blues

William Handy interpreted the unwritten music of his people for the world, but he didn't start out with that in mind. A successful band leader and composer, he also managed a dozen dance bands and employed over sixty musicians when a note was passed up to him during a performance, "Would you play some of your own native music?"

As Handy tells it in his autobiography "Father of the Blues," "This baffled me. The men in this group could not 'fake it' or 'sell it' like minstrel men. They were all musicians and bowed strictly to the authority of printed notes." They played a southern melody and a second note was passed up, "Would you object if our local colored band played a few dances?"

The newcomers, three seedy looking boys with guitar, mandolin and worn-out bass, began a haunting, over and over strain that had no clear beginning or ending, the kind of music he'd heard all his life but, in his words "was kept in the back rooms of my mind while the parlor was reserved for dressed-up music." While listening to the country boys, he wondered if people would pay money to hear such music. "The answer was not long in coming. A rain of silver dollars began to fall around their feet..the dancers went wild, more money than my nine musicians were getting paid for the entire engagement."

That night the blues were witnessed by Handy and came to light. "I saw the beauty of primitive music. They had the stuff the people wanted. It touched the spot..those country black boys at Cleveland (Mississippi) had taught me something that could not possibly have been gained from books, something that would, however, cause books to be written. Art, in the highbrow sense, was not in my mind. My idea of what constitutes music was changed by the sight of that silver money cascading around the splayed feet of a Mississippi string band."

Within a day or two, he'd orchestrated a number of local tunes, including, "The Last Shot Got Him," "Your Clock Ain't Right," and "Make Me a Pallet On Your Floor."

In 1911, he wrote "Memphis Blues" and published it himself since the big publishers didn't want it. Among the sixty songs he wrote, "St. Louis Blues" is probably his most well-known but, to his mind, "Beale Street" has the most interesting history. He wrote the song after meeting a dog-tired piano player who played from seven at night until seven in the morning in a cheap bar, resting himself by playing with alternate hands. Handy set the man's life story down in notes. "I have tried to write history, to crystallize a form for the colored workman's personal music, just as the spirituals give form to his religious convictions."

Lessons From Early Cowboys

Lamperti's vocal style descended from the Italian's Golden Age of Song, by word of mouth. We have an example of word-of-mouth singers from our own culture that the old master would

Blacks made the church their own through song.
Author Alice Walker
during a live interview on
public radio

One time I heard Judy Collins on the car radio. They were playing the song that she does with the whales. It was so beautiful I had to drive to the side of the road. I couldn't drive anymore. There were tears in my eyes.
Cynthia Gooding, leading female
folk singer in fifties and early
sixties; her radio show introduced
Bob Dylan to the public

53

have appreciated: a society of men who took off on their own as teenagers and pursued singular lives; spent hours and hours of solitude necessary to get into the contemplative self; learned songs by heart; appreciated music and good singers; had the proper stance for singing and were not afraid to have a go at it.

I am talking about the American cowboy, not the shoot-em-up cowboys of movies, but cowhands who wouldn't dream of taking a gun on trail (too heavy) and were too poor to own horses. Today few such cowhands exist, but in the early years of this century it was common for a young fellow to follow the cowboy trade.

Over a period of fifteen years, beginning in 1970, I hung out with a half dozen of the old hands, getting the story of the working cowhand on tape and on the backs of envelopes and napkins. There are many lessons to be learned from these men; the one that applies to our emotional well being is simple. We become what we desire. We all know unhappy people who desired nothing more than wealth and attained it. The cowhands desired freedom, and a life on horseback.

Lesson number two: our thoughts dictate what we are. If we see ourselves as singers, we sing. The early cowhands didn't necessarily grow up on horseback but heard about cowboying from dime novels popular in the late 1800's and early 1900's. Whether they lived in Norway, Scotland or Pennsylvania, they thought about becoming cowboys until it became who they were. Love of horses was a big thing, even if they had never seen one.

"How'd you know you'd love horses?"

My question would be received with an embarrassed grin. "I just knew." Tony Grace had never been on a horse (except on a Milwaukee merry-go-round) but worked his way west on the railroad in 1907 at age 17 and lived the life of a cowhand. Art Wahl came alone from Norway at fourteen. He'd only seen big

Just about every popular singer, concert artist, and orchestra of the day gave widespread exposure in 1933 to "Home on the Range," a little-known folk song of the West (discovered by ballad collector John Lomax in San Antonio in 1908). Live radio broadcasts on all principal networks gave it a popularity never before attained by an American song...Also in 1933, Billy Hill's immortal composition "The Last Round-Up" hit the radio air waves. With the help of pulp westerns, Zane Grey novels, radio broadcasts, sound movies, and the unprecedented outpouring of new cowboys songs during the next ten years, all America was singing, humming or enjoying cowboy and western songs.

Jim Bob Tinsley,
"A Cowboy Has to Sing"

workhorses but, like Tony, he just knew he was going to take to horses. While nosing around the Montana State archives in Helena, I came upon a stack of handwritten index cards from a reunion of pioneering cowboys who came west in the late 1800's, a decade or so before Tony and Art (who, by the way, lived to ages 100 and 105). The men came as teenagers from all over the world, few had ever seen a horse.

They just knew.

As studies of the brain become more sophisticated, a fact of human nature becomes more apparent: we are what we think we are. A generation of boys became cowhands. If you see yourself as a singer, that is what you will become.

Why Cowboys Sang

The cowhand's life wasn't shoot-em-up like the dime novel portrayed. The aspiring cowboy would purchase a wide-brimmed hat and saddle, hop on a train, sign on with an outfit, draw his string of horses from the remuda and ride out. Riding out meant months on horseback during spring and fall roundups, usually alone or with a partner out of earshot, a job Tony termed "cow chaperone."

"Handle 'em easy," he said, "Keep 'em quiet."

It was a young man's job (the few who kept at it until forty didn't settle down and marry until then) done not for money but for freedom. The freedom got to these boys.

Out of this real experience came music unique to America. The cowboy song. Not the country western that goes along with fancy chaps and cowboy hats but trail songs, story songs, tell-it-like-it-is songs. The only other examples of wholely

Wilf Carter, in stage-cowboy getup in the 1930s, billed himself as the "Yodeling Cowboy" before he became "Montana Slim."
Courtesy of Jeanette Ziesemer

American music are blues, jazz, Black spirituals, and barbershop quartets.

In 1982, I collected the best of the old songs and poems for a Montana Folk Life Project. Tracking down songs was fun. The director of the project and I made our way across the state, looking for men who had grown up in the ranch tradition and learned songs by ear.

My purpose here is not to discuss the songs they sang (look in the bibliography for cowboy songbooks), but the way they sang them. These were men willing to sit down and sing from the heart. They knew all the old poems and had nothing against Shakespeare. I kept up contact with several of them through the mail and found they were willing to draw a picture to illustrate a point.

Draw, sing, recite poetry?

My private theory has always been that the lonesome hours spent on horseback under the changing sky allowed these men access to what I have attempted to describe in the beginning of this chapter: the altered state of consciousness, the creative self, the right side of the brain. I knew them in their eighties and nineties, and they hadn't lost it.

Paul Young is an example. When I met him in 1982, he was nearing ninety, a slight wisp of a man who needed a cane, two hearing aids and bottle-glass bifocals to navigate. Raised in Utah by a mother who wanted her bright son to become an engineer, he broke his first bronc at age thirteen and by eighteen had cowboyed his way to Montana. During a taping session that lasted until midnight, Paul would break into song while describing trail drives of the generation of cowboys who preceded him. His voice was hearty and robust, not the voice of a frail old man. He was tireless— "A ky-yi-yippie, yippie-yea, yippie-yea," he sang, and explained that this oldest trail song— "Old Chisholm Trail"—had a verse for every state between Montana and Texas. Typical of most old hands, he considered

We've just been joined by one of my favorite yodelers, Patsy Montana, who had a big hit in 1935--first million selling single for a woman in country music, "I Wanna Be a Cowboy's Sweetheart."
Kathy Fink on her
"Learn to Yodel" tape

The seeds of Western music were often planted by men whose roots had long been in the soil..predominantly Irish. The black man's music was adapted to a society (the blues) whereas the Irishman's was adapted to a terrain. The melodies were often left intact, but they had great elasticity and, when stretched and slowed, fitted very well with the gait of a walking or trotting cow pony.
Katie Lee

trail songs his favorite. "You can always tell a trail song, it has lilt, sort of a feeling like you're on horseback. The rhythm goes with the riding." He stretched the singing-talking history lesson way back to Mexico in the 1500's when, he said, Queen Isabella of Spain sent a thousand horsemen to the New World. When he forgot a stanza, he created his own.

A Personal Songbag

From the cowboys, I learned the importance of collecting songs. Printed neatly on the neck of Glenn Ohrlin's guitar is a long list of songs. It's Glenn's songbag. He knows the words and melodies to each song. When he comes across a new song that strikes his fancy, into the songbag it goes.

Glenn—rodeo cowboy, Arkansas rancher and author of a cowboy songbook, "The Hellbound Train,"—is a popular performer at folk festivals and on college campuses. I met him at a folk festival in St. Louis. My job was to chaperone Kenny and Verna Trowbridge from the small town of Darby, Montana, to Missouri. Glenn parked his bedroll in the same home where we were put up, and I became the lucky onlooker in late night popcorn-munching, lie-swapping, song-exchanging session between Glenn and Kenny. In those days, I was often called on to introduce the cowboys at festivals, or to play the part of the dummie at a story-swapping session, but I didn't see myself as a singer. I did, however, learn a lot of songs by listening and some of them have become part of my personal songbag.

There's a national network of cowboys like Glenn who are into performing for the fun of it. Seventy-three year old Kenny, new to the circuit, had a motherlode of original material. Glenn, a born collector of cowboy lore, was delighted with the new stuff. Lack of professional jealousy among cowboy-entertainers is heartening. Songs, stories and poems are out of their mouths and into circulation. One of the songs Glenn sang that night was "Boomer Johnson," the story of one hand's retribution against a murderous cook given to such actions as punching his six-shooter

For a cowboy has to sing
And a cowboy has to yell,
Or his heart would break inside of him
At the gate of the home corral.
by Bob Nolan, 1939,
from "A Cowboy Has to Sing"
by Jim Bob Tinsley

Everybody loved French opera star Emma Calve. During her first trip across the U.S. in the 1890's, she traveled in a special railroad car with a group from the Metropolitan Opera. They were met in Houston, a small town in those days, by 300 cowboys who had gathered from all over the country. Calve sang a lively Spanish tune and the cowboys whooped and shouted their approval. As the train pulled away, many of the cowboys raced alongside as fast as they could go. "The last we saw of them," Calve said, "was a thick cloud of dust beside the railroad track in our wake."

From *Famous Women Singers* by Homer Ulrich

Stick to the oldies. In thirty years when someone makes a request, you'll reach back and remember the words.

Jo Rainbolt

through rock-hard doughnuts and into a cowboy's belly while saying "Yer eatin' some." "Boomer" became Kenny's personal favorite. When he and Glenn later joined other cowhands on a national "Old Puncher's Reunion" sponsored by the National Council for the Traditional Arts, I saw grown men and women (including a group of nuns) hold their sides and weep at Kenny's rendition of "Boomer."

How to Memorize Songs

Kenny was bad at names (except, of course, the names of horses). He was always bawling at me, "Fer Crissake, what's that guy's name? The one from Oklahoma with the poem I want to learn?" He caught on to my first name but never did learn to spell it (gave it an e on the end) and failed completely with my last name. When he introduced me as his sidekick at folk shows, he gave my name a creative twist. Sometimes I was Jo Rambo. But no one picked up a song quicker than Kenny.

All the old hands have an uncanny ability to memorize songs. Schooling wasn't an important part of their backgrounds, memorization was. If they came from the ranching tradition, they picked up poems, stories and songs as kids from listening to older hands. If they came West as teenagers or young men, they picked up the knack around the campfire. There wasn't much for entertainment. Contrary to what the movies show, there were no guitars in camp. A harmonica might be stashed in the bedroll or in the grain bag the men stored their few possessions in, but nothing as big and fragile as a guitar. The human voice meant a lot, for stories and for song.

Overall, it was a quieter time. This made memorization easier. The moment Kenny heard "Boomer," he began to learn it. Once a song or poem is learned, it sticks. It's amazing how the songs are retained. Time and again, I've heard a song requested from the audience and, after a moment of head scratching, an old hand will come out with all the words to something he hasn't heard for fifty years. Of course, I hadn't heard it either, so I shouldn't say "all the words." These old hands were creative, always making something do for something else (a million uses for rawhide and neckerchiefs), and not above making up whole stanzas if memory fails, or just for the fun of it.

We Can Learn to Listen

There's an art to listening. Turn off the TV. Focus your attention. Don't pretend interest if you're not interested (that's another art). Reynaldo Hahn, the gifted Frenchman introduced earlier, urged his audience of singers to listen to everyday sounds, to "glean information from every corner," and used the example of his friend, the renowned composer Stravinksy, "the slightest resonance or vibration arouses his attention; a fork striking the glass, a cane lightly touching a chair, the rustle of a silken cloth, the grating of a door, the sound of footsteps."

Cowboy Tony paid that kind of attention to detail, and his attention deepened as his eyes weakened after age 100. "Sit down and tell me about it!" he'd demand after one of my whirlwind shoestring trips to Mexico or Southeast Alaska. The old hands listened to each other with the same intensity. Words meant something. Stories meant something. Songs recorded all of it.

More on Memorization

It's a good idea to commit songs to memory. When I sing without looking at the words and notes, I find I put more feeling into the song. It's as if I'm telling myself a story. A trick I use for memorization is to depend on that story.

For some reason (probably because I seldom listen to commercial radio) I have never heard Bette Midler sing her popular song "The Rose." My voice teacher gave me the lyrics

The cowboy tradition continued when the homesteaders moved in and farming replaced huge ranches. More diversity in ethnic music arrived with them, and long hours alone behind plows pulled by teams or tractors were made more bearable by singing. My brothers (in their mid-70's) still remember all the words to songs like 'Ivan Skavinsky Skvaar,' 'On the Bum Again,' 'Smokey Mountain Bill,' 'Darling Clementine' and dozens of other old and newer songs. Railroad songs were big, too, 'Wreck of the Old '97,' 'John Henry,' etc.

Liz Fee, editor,
singer, neighbor

The mind is busy learning more activities than the intellectual side is aware of—every time you hear a piece of music you learn more than you think.

Bonnie Jean Triplett

59

The folk craze of the early '60's...helped pump new life into the careers of country blues stylists such as Honeyboy Edwards and Muddy Waters. Soon they were all enjoying record, club, concert and television success patronized by a wide-eyed and eager young, white audience of blues fans worldwide.

George Hansen in an article on Honeyboy Edwards in *Acoustic Guitar* magazine

which I learned for a friend's engagement party. I sang it as a story and, afterwards, another friend who is a disc jockey commented that she had heard the song many times but had never before listened to the words.

A memorization trick I learned from Kenny is to pay more attention to the last stanzas of a song. The first part is often familiar enough to glide through (besides, we have the audience's attention). If you go over and over the ending, you'll feel renewed interest coming from within yourself rather than a sigh of relief.

In our home, we have a wonderful selection of tapes, records and CDs but I am most excited by public radio because I never know what I might hear next. Sometimes a song stirs my heart and I have to sit down and listen, or I might dance, or cry. Until I began voice lessons, it never entered my head to take those songs as my own and learn them. It was different when I was a kid. I'd con my younger brother into doing the rowing in a rickety wooden boat on a nearby lake by singing to him. Show tunes, hymns, spirituals. When pressed, I still remember those old songs.

Country Versus Cowboy, and Don't Forget the Irish

This is probably as good a time as any to clear up confusion (usually from outside the West) about country western and cowboy songs. They are not the same. Cowboy songs almost always told a story, often a parody on life— sometimes sad, often funny. Songs from outside the cow camp were often included in a cowpoke's songbag (for instance: "I'll Be With You When the Roses Bloom Again," "Letter Edged in Black," "I'm a Rambler, I'm a Gambler"). Cowboys didn't sing about broken-hearted love affairs (a popular theme in Country Western), but songs often involved sweetness towards Mother. This doesn't surprise me since many of the old hands of my acquaintance had left home as young teenagers to escape ornery fathers and stepfathers and never did get over sympathy for their long-gone mothers.

Songs reflected pride in the outfit. I've come across penciled versions of well-known trail songs where the C-K's, the LU Bars or the 79's were extolled as "the best." An early cowboy didn't work for an outfit he couldn't be proud of. If a fellow had reason to bad mouth his boss or fellow workers, he should quit. They weren't working for money (twenty or thirty bucks a month including grub and a place to lay out a bedroll), but for the freedom of being on horseback in wide open country. Songs reflect this feeling of closeness to the land.

Bless the Irish: a rollicking, gifted, big hearted, musical bunch of people. The tunes that early immigrants brought from Ireland are the ones we hear not only in cowboy songs but in some of our best-loved American folk songs. The Irish came into this country, adapted to any number of jobs, and changed their songs to fit the work and the terrain.

"Pa was only one of the immigrants who poured into the country during the 19th century," singer Katie Lee wrote in her book about cowboys, "They worked on railroads, planted potatoes, fought in saloons, mined and sang."

Her father moved Westward with the Union Pacific Railroad as a terrier—"Drill ye terriers drill!" When the transcontinental railroad was completed in Utah in 1869, he traded in pick and shovel for spurs and chaps and drove cattle north.

A lot of immigrants became cowboys this way. What singled out the Irish was flexibility. "The Cornish, Welsh, Chinese and German kept their language, held to tradition," Katie Lee wrote "while the Irish cowboy changed the names of places in Ireland to the new towns in the West (i.e. "the flower of Belton, the Rose of Saline" in "I'm a Rambler, I'm a Gambler").

Kenny was Irish and knew as many Irish ballads as he did cowboy songs. But then, the two go hand-in-hand.

Who decided rock was all about kids? When it started, it was rhythm and blues, black people's music. They wouldn't have said it was for kids. I learned from coming together with John that the rock beat simulates our heartbeat: that's why the music is so powerful. So I think rock is for all people with heartbeats.

Yoko Ono, 63

The kind of music that's always appealed to me—songs about pain, love, release, hunger, and loneliness—has nothing to do with age. In fact, your experience of those feelings and, consequently, your music, grows richer with time...when I'm onstage I feel really juicy and powerful. So, when I'm eighty I want to do just what I'm doing now.

Singer Bonnie Raitt

Too Many Dead Cowboys

"THERE IS A BIG BAR STOOL
IN THE SKY
WHERE ALL DRINKERS GO
WHEN THEY DIE.
BAR BILLS ARE A THING
OF THE PAST
AND ONE'S CHECKS STOP
BOUNCING AT LAST."

My neighbor in the Bitterroot Valley, Earsel Bloxham, sang the old songs straight from his heart. He was seventy but looked fifty, wore a Gene Autry-style felt and had the kindest face I've ever seen. He sang with a twang, a downhome sound that made me feel nostalgic. But that effect wasn't universal. After a moving rendition by Earsel of "There's an Empty Cot in the Bunkhouse Tonight," 89-year old Joe Hughes turned to me and said "Too many dead cowboys."

The comment made me laugh, for it was prime Joe, who disliked anything that characterized his youthful wild Irish cowhand days as sentimental. I'm sentimental about the old hands, but I agree with Glenn Ohrlin who said writers are overly keen to remark on the sadness of cowboy songs. "Seems to me a lot more are comical," he drawled.

Away from the drudgery and long hours of roundup, they knew how to play. And that's what we're after.

Folk Music

In 1961—the year singers like Bob Dylan, Joan Baez and Peter, Paul and Mary introduced America to the folk scene, I went from Wisconsin to New York where it was happening. I didn't know it was happening, my desire was to go to Europe, and New York seemed the likely jumping-off place. I roomed in Queens with a Chilean woman I'd met in Milwaukee, took the subway downtown to work in a restaurant, and stashed my tips in quart jars for that trip to Europe. It was summer and, looking back, it seems a time of innocence. Of the definitions for innocence in my dictionary, I choose number five: lack of understanding or knowledge. None of us knew what was happening, we just did it. It would be ten years before the nation woke up to Watergate and the escalation of bombing raids in Vietnam. I felt totally alive and, more than that, safe in the audacity and raw energy of New York. The city seemed washed with music and sun. I was poor but money wasn't a big deal in those days. I kept watching those tips grow and spent my time wandering the streets. Beats (who looked old to me) read poetry in Washington Square, and young singers strummed songs that have become classics. At home, I'd heard Pete Seeger and Peter, Paul and Mary (everybody had), and twisted with Elvis at high school dances; I probably heard some future greats on street corners of Greenwich Village and didn't even know it.

It was a sweet time, not just for me but for the nation. The media hadn't yet brought our awareness to the level where even wars are televised live. We didn't yet feel it was our job to set things right. Things happened without us knowing ahead of time, which is lovely. The folk scene happened, a movement that wasn't new but was grounded in traditional folk and the blues.

Folk City

Folk singers from all over the country and Canada migrated to New York that year. Folk was happening in a blue collar bar and restaurant called "Folk City." The gnome-like owner, an Italian named Mike Porco, liked music and had good business instincts. He booked the traditionalists and was the only club owner to pay the new breed money for singing. Folk City wasn't much of a club—a light bulb with a metal tube shining down on a five foot stage, but it had an unpretentious downstairs dressing room where songs were debuted, historic connections made and careers shaped. Porco didn't know folk; he relied on his gut instincts while booking singers. Writer and musicologist Robert Shelton helped by recommending acts and reviewing them for the New York Times (a favorable review brought bookings with Ed Sullivan and the big clubs).

Hoyt Axton has settled in the Bitterroot--the rural Montana valley south of Missoula where I lived for 20 years and raised my kids--but he was one of the young singers who migrated to New York in the sixties from places like Minnesota and

I get tired of people thinking folk singers did something wrong and passed out of favor...pop music just by its very definition must always be in a state of flux. Folk music is fundamentally classical, just like traditional jazz or classical music. It's a root form of music and has times when it is popular and less popular...Peter, Paul and Mary's music hasn't changed. I don't think it's necessary to change.

Mary Travers

I came to the Village because that's where it was happening. That's where the music was, that's where my kind of people were. The first night I went there, I didn't know anybody. I went straight to Gerdes (Folk City). For me, in those days, Folk City was Mecca. It was the place. There was no other. It was where it was happening.

Hoyt Axton

"OKAY, YOU GOT ME, OFFICER! I'M A SALESMAN FOR A *HEARING AID COMPANY*. WHEN I SING I TURN THE AMPLIFIER UP SO LOUD IT RUINS PEOPLE'S EARDRUMS."

Rock & roll is so close to universal because it can adapt so quickly to new environments. The music was destined to change with each new place it encountered. The British added to the mix as they adapted it, as did New Yorkers and West Indians and poets and millionaires and punks.

Bill Flanagan

California. They came to listen and to learn from the traditional folk singers and, in keeping with the times, they quickly veered off into their own unique styles. The folk process, an art as natural as breathing, encourages this: the singer takes in a song, masters it, and allows it to flow in a personal style. Some traditionalists were annoyed by the experimentation of the sixties while others appreciated the influx of new talent. As pointed out by George Hansen in an article in *Acoustic Guitar* about the legendary blues musician David "Honeyboy" Edwards (still performing in his eighties), the sixties introduced American folk to the world and created a wider audience for the older keepers of songs.

"The folk craze of the early '60's...helped pump new life into the careers of country blues stylists such as Honeyboy Edwards and Muddy Waters," Hansen wrote, "Soon they were all enjoying record, club, concert and television success patronized by a wide-eyed and eager, young, white audience of blues fans worldwide."

Lotte Lehmann (1888-1976) German Soprano

Chapter Four
Your Turn

Author Jo Rainbolt and Salish singer Chuck Hunter sing a final hymn during a rousing memorial service for "Cowboy Fred" Haydon, May, 1997.

Photo by Lee Zimmerman

We've read enough about singers and creativity, it's time to sing. But, before we get into the nuts and bolts of how, when and where to do it, there are still a few spooks lurking in the background, ready to trip us up.

The First of Three Spooks: Shame

Skills have been presented to give you wings. If you're afraid to begin (even by yourself, in the shower or the car) it might be because someone has said you can't.

I am aware of the creative process and how tender it is. It frustrated me when parents arrived to sign up children for my summer art classes with two or more kids in tow. Invariably, one would be singled out as "the artist in the family," or "the one who can draw." All kids are artists. Those labeled nonartists at home thrived in the freewheeling atmosphere of my workshop. Some did better than their talented sibling. The emphasis was on messy stuff—clay, finger painting, tie dying, making candles in the sand by the river. I am not denying inborn talent. My kids all created wonderful art objects while growing up, but Kori could draw and had an uncanny sense of color and how to fill up the page. She was the artist. Sadly, I did to her in music what other parents did to their kids in art.

We were not a singing family but we loved music and the kids heard plenty of it. It wasn't unusual for them to write, produce and act out plays that included songs. The two little girls could sing. By this, I mean they had the ability to hear songs and reproduce them. Kori and my oldest stepdaughter Tahlia were labeled nonsingers. We did not encourage them to sing. I am afraid we encouraged them to stick to the speaking parts.

Yet, these two older girls have a fervent love of music as adults (reminding me of book-loving friends who do not write). Tahlia has an expert's ear and has introduced me to some of my favorite female vocalists. Kori is the kind of listener every

As small children, most of us listened to music with our entire bodies, charming parents and aunts and uncles with our free and joyous movement. But charming our relatives can be dangerous. Their encouragement can sow the seeds of self consciousness. When a natural response turns into a performance, the charm fades and we may be scolded for showing off. Alas, spontaneity and scolding can become cousins in our minds.

Eloise Ristad from her book
A Soprano on Her Head

performer picks out in a crowd. Her clear blue eyes send sparks clear across the room when I sing a new song for her. Recently I repeated my apology for not encouraging her to sing as a child. She laughed and assured me she doesn't need to sing. Kori skis down cliffs and rides bareback with the ease of a cat, feeds elk in her Idaho yard and has the most vivid night dreams of any person I know. The tedium of law school drained her as an artist, but I am certain she will take up art again the same way I returned to singing.

She's right, she doesn't need to sing. I used her and Tahlia as examples: the creative process is tender and thrives with encouragement. It is kept alive by desire, not talent. Music and art, a big part of being human, comes from the heart.

The Next Spook: Silencing the Inner Critic

I think of it as a wall because it feels like one, sometimes it's more of a curtain than a wall, always heavy and seemingly impenetrable. It makes it hard for me to breathe, I feel sluggish, often I go for a walk, but all it really takes is to get writing, or drawing or singing. The wall is in truth a bully without any brawn, ready to give in at the first sign of artistic energy, it is the voice of a market economy that hammers the relentless message: get smart, get a real job, make money, you're doing WHAT? Singing? Drawing? Painting a picture? When you could be...and of course the list of couldas and shouldas is endless.

What is this inner voice that tells us that any endeavor, creative or otherwise, is doomed without serious attention to detail? That singing cannot be play? That messing with clay or paints is not art unless it looks like something? That writing random thoughts in a journal is a waste of time, and simply sitting and looking inward is day dreaming and bad?

In other words, where does the voice come from that insists life should be a grind?

I write a great deal about how crucial is it to give ourselves permission to fail—to make mistakes—and how important it is to send our judges off temporarily on a chartered bus when we begin to experiment.

Eloise Ristad

I'm willing to guess that it is not just the voice of a market society saying "work, work, work," but a combination of voices—the parent who silenced our questions, the teacher who was less than enthusiastic about our art, the older sibling who poked fun at a stick drawing.

I was lucky. My mom called me an artist and brought me peanut butter sandwiches on a tray when I messed around with mud and paint in the basement but, still, a high school science teacher scoffed at impressionistic water colors the art teacher encouraged me to do and his words "I thought you could do better than that" overpowered the art teacher's praise.

The voice that says "I thought you could do better" is only trying to help, but it is the kind of help that kills the initial stage of any creative project. When I sit down to a clean page on the typewriter, I tell the voice to move over. Time for you later, Busy Body.

I call it Busy Body, or Buster, but with a note of respect since the voice has a point: I can do better. But not in the beginning. Beginnings need light and freedom, beginnings need a sense of play, which might explain why little kids are so good at jumping in and doing it. Sometimes I set a manuscript aside for six months, or a year, and then I invite the critical voice to come help me read what I have written.

Singing is play for me. Why get serious? I'm doing this for me, for fun, for ease. Still, the inner voice, the wall, waits in the wings, ready to trip me up. Warmups help. La, la, la, up and down the scale. The critical voice quickly gets bored while ignored.

Sometimes it's necessary to call on inner warriors to help us out. I am tall but not heavy and while learning a difficult art song in German (Der Lindenbaum by Schubert) my teacher said "Imagine you have a barrel of breath below the rib cage to call on." I went one step further and imagined I was as stocky as my

We didn't have a radio, we didn't need one. The four of us kids sang all the time—we'd throw the soapy dishrag at each other and sing and yodel. Poor Mother would be ready to kill us. "Would you kids please do that hollering outside?" Then under her breath she'd mumble, "I guess it beats fighting."

Theresa Collum
singer, pianist, guitarist, and
yodeler who entertains residents at
the nursing home in
Hot Springs, Montana.

The singer needs to get into the place and do it, then the artistry comes in—the mind doesn't have to think anymore. Natural aspects of the voice are what we want, not what's taken on by imitation or affectation.

Bonnie Jean Triplett

own great-grandmother Anna, a woman I never met but whose stalwart girth and calm wide face on an old photo has always intrigued me. I don't know if Grandma Anna sang, but she certainly helps me out.

She had to have a tough life, coming penniless from Norway with a brother in her early twenties, working on shipboard as a nurse, but the other thing I admired about her in that old photo is the twinkle in her eye. It's obvious she knew how to have fun.

Perhaps this is what we need: a sense of play. Perhaps that's all we've lost. To sing is to be fully awake in the moment, to let go and play.

Spook Three: Authority

Opening up the creative spaces within ourselves can be frightening. It requires letting go of parts of ourselves that serve as the voices of authority. Anyone who has given up a relationship with a person who served as an authority figure knows how unsettling it is. We have all done this because we have all left home. No matter how gentle mother or father was, it's confusing to be without the habit of a voice telling us this-is-the-way-it-is.

We cannot, however, put the burden of authority on Mom, boss, boyfriend. The outside voice merely acts as a substitute for our own inner voice, always ready to tell us what to do, or more likely, what not to do. To be creative requires a constant dialogue with oneself, giving worth, pats on the back, encouragement. The best teachers find the best in us and encourage it. We can become our own best teachers.

With proper use of the breath we can begin to sing at once, but the creative space inside ourselves needs to be carefully tended before we can expect to sing joyfully. The first year I gardened in my new yard, I placed the seeds in the ground with no preparation, the results were edible but puny compared to my neighbor's produce. That fall I prepared the ground—covered the garden with dry manure and old straw and had it tilled under in the spring. The resulting harvest of beets and carrots was as big and bountiful as my neighbors.

I've mentioned that I tell my own critical voice to move over, time for you later, but this only works if I am already in a creative state of mind (a state that is not magical but comes from regular output). After a dry spell, the critical voice will not easily be told to move over. Lethargy sets in. Hours might be put in at a regular job, but to sing or dance or paint takes too much effort. A certain tenderness with self is important during fallow times. Such time is not wasted space. We are simply getting ready to produce. Read good books, take long walks, give the soul a gentle watering.

Stage fright—concentrate on what you are doing instead of how. Turn fright into focus, concentration, intensity. Pavarotti does five deep breaths before going on stage.
Bonnie Jean Triplett

Honesty With Oneself

What if every time we voice a criticism towards another person it is aimed at ourself? This could very well be the way it happens, given the complexity of human nature, but the point is—imagine how all that angry response to others (which eventually turns inward) feeds the critical voice within. When I am in a habit of writing or sculpting or singing, I turn a gentle eye on the world. I do not need to feed my inner demons. They bow down to clarity, as do all the other forces of the universe.

Clarity is a better word than honesty. We all try to be honest but the word is easily misconstrued. As children we say "honest, Mom, I didn't do it" with our fingers crossed behind our backs (and take a look at where this leads with our "honest" politicians). Honesty these days too often implies a personal morality, as in see-what-a-good-person-I-am. Not that it isn't a good word in the old fashioned sense: honesty towards the earth, the elders and oneself.

I was never able to sing until I sang in the sweat lodge. Everyone else was singing and I felt like I'd literally die if I didn't participate. It took me years to step out of who I am on the outside and truly participate. I'm still on the shy side.
Gary Le Deau, Arlee, Montana

I live on an Indian reservation and my debt is to the elders. From them I've learned another meaning of honesty, plain and unadorned, the opposite of the modern notion of acting

71

Songs and dreams? I live by them.
Kootenai elder Louie Gingras

respectable in order to impress others and have a good reputation. To the elders, word means something. Word means everything because words express what is in the heart.

Choices

While singing, we either find the place to sing in— high, wide and open—or we don't. It takes a certain kind of energy to silence the inner critic and make sounds that might sound foolish until we get it. I've already mentioned that to feel foolish is part of the creative process; we are stepping aside from the way things are usually done and risk being laughed at. As modern Americans, we expect results. "Production" is a big word in our vocabulary. It takes a leap to open up to the way we feel while singing, rather than the way we sound.

We are creatures of habit. But, regardless of our conditioning, we do have choices. We don't have to be victims of a hurry up society's sense of time. We can make a conscious decision to breathe a little deeper and make room for our creative selves. The alternative is to hurry along until we die. Still, the impulse of self protection is a powerful one. We don't want to stand out from society, to be labeled different, so we turn instinctively towards what others find correct. Who are the others? That depends on who we are, what we are used to, who we think is watching our behavior. As a child, I heard my mother mention "they" and what they might think, but when I asked her who they were, she didn't have a ready answer. I was about ten and remember thinking, so there is no they. Kids are far smarter than we give them credit for. Remember the story of the emperor's new clothes? No one dared comment on his nakedness, perhaps they believed he was grandly clothed (the power of like-mindedness) until a child exclaimed over it. I doubted the they, or I wouldn't have asked about it. Come to think of it, ten is about the age we start believing in the power of them and let go of our own wise intuition.

Trust the child, and be reminded that the fear we feel when trying something new is not a bad thing. Fear and the pain that goes along with it are avoided at all costs in modern society, but they are messengers moving us through the dark, leading us towards the possibility of a sudden awakening, a pure flash of understanding.

We have all had sudden losses where we cannot run or hide. Confronted by pain, overcome with grief, we also experience a heightened awareness, a feeling of elation mixed with the loss. Is this why men make war? To feel fully alive?

Perhaps in a society where creative needs were met, there would be no need for war.

I am not advocating suffering. Self-love, not suffering, is the mother of creativity. The worst agony is self-reproach. Fear and pain can lead us towards the light. Self-reproach creates a void that can only be filled with suffering. As long as we draw breath, we have the choice.

It would be difficult for a human being to live an unrhythmic life, for rhythm is inherent in too many bodily processes—the beat of the heart, breathing, peristalsis. Even though we might not be consciously aware of these rhythms, they form a backdrop or undercurrent for our consciousness, waking and sleeping.

Eloise Ristad

Performance

If the idea of singing causes you great anxiety, it's most likely because it is confused with performance. Some people never get over performance anxiety. There is always the option of singing for yourself and not performing. Remember Rosa Ponselle from the first chapter? Hailed as the world's finest soprano, she never got over her dread of appearing in public. Opera lovers wailed when she stepped down at forty, but she happily continued singing for herself for twenty years.

I made a deal with myself to sing "The Rose" at my best pal's bachelorette party. The hostess said bring a love poem to share. I decided on a song instead, and one that most folks remember as Bette Midler's. How to make it mine? The words were appropriate: love is a flower, you its only seed. Fifteen years ago, after Libby divorced, I sent her a card with frog seeds;

Since I grew up singing with my brothers, I never experienced performance anxiety until I sang alone on stage. Dance bands didn't count since nobody was staring at me. One way I coped was to always begin on the right key. I don't read notes so it meant listening closely. Another was to imagine the audience naked. But what worked best was finding a sympathetic face in the audience, someone who clearly enjoyed my singing, and return to that face.

Liz Fee

included with the card were directions: water the seeds and someday a prince will come. I found I couldn't sing this simple song and do it well. The easy songs are hardest. The Italian art songs and Schubert's German songs that I sing during my weekly lesson force me to attention—let go and breathe or die. But my mind made light of "The Rose" (possibly to hide my fear of performing). Why try for the technique? I sang before I took lessons didn't I? Do it like a poem, my teacher advised, and keep your musical phrases long and on the breath.

Walking by myself, I sang it over and over until a light bulb went off. It was the first two words that tripped me up. "Some say.." I hate "s" sounds while singing and my "o" is never placed right. I pronounce "some" like "sum." I asked a visiting French house painter to pronounce "some" for me and he obliged, didn't even ask why. It's ommm, a meditative sound not ummm.

What's in a single vowel? All the difference.

"Sommm say..." became my mantra.

I have a great time performing, but I'm not sure I want to do it forever..It's very alluring—there's nothing quite like it when everybody stands up and goes mad. So, although I love it, I always want to keep in my mind that there's another life where that doesn't happen and it's just as valuable.

Rock star Marianne Faithful

The night of the party my knees were shaking. I promised myself I'd do it before dinner but lost courage. During the delicious main course, I kept telling myself I didn't have to sing (my daughter Kristen and a close friend were the only guests who knew my intention). It wasn't until after the sumptuous dessert that I drew a big breath, pushed my chair away from the table and told the frog-seed story. "Sommm say" got me started and I guess I made it all the way through the song. All I remember is keeping my eyes on lithe dark-eyed Libby. She was always radiant and that night she glowed. Our friendship was forged in nature. My mind skipped to skinny-dipping in icy mountain lakes, Libby swimming eye-to-eye to a bachelor beaver. She was marrying an outdoor guy, a sweetheart, a prince. I don't think I sang well but fourteen women were beaming at me from around the table when I'd finished.

Libby's heart gave out unexpectedly and she died in her sleep last August after four months of what can only be described as married bliss; at her memorial service by the Blackfoot River, her sister told me that she'd never forget me singing to Libby at her bachelorette party.

A Public Performance

Some people get along fine without ever performing. Others want to get it out there. My first public solo took place last summer during a festival in Thompson Falls, a rural community of three thousand people. I'd listened to Patsy Cline's "I Can't Help It If I Am Still In Love With You" until I had it memorized and that's the song I chose to solo with.

Listening to tapes is a good way to learn a song, but be certain to practice without the tape if you intend to sing it alone. I was lucky enough to practice with an experienced guitar player. David Little was new to our town, a real pro with a complete sound system, plus his voice and guitar skills rivaled those of the Canadian folk singer Gordon Lightfoot. He agreed to join a small group of us at the Thompson Falls event and to practice my song with me. We arranged to meet the day before the event.

PASSING THRU—
PASSING THRU;
SOMETIMES
HAPPY-SOMETIMES
BLUE ...

(FROM OLD FOLK SONG)

By the time I arrived at the practice, my mind was reeling with excuses—it was too soon, I'd always push myself, I wasn't singing to prove anything to anybody but to please myself, there was plenty of other music for the program, I was already singing a duet with my music teacher at the event, and so on. I rambled all this to David who was concentrating on adjusting knobs on his PA system and tuning his guitar. The man was all business. I completed my litany by telling David thanks-for-your-time and was ready to bolt for the door. He handed me a set of earphones and said. "Ready?" His next question is a killer for me. "What key?"

Forget about the accuracy of your rhythm and connect your body with music in any way that feels comfortable. See how you come to life...locked up emotions can begin to release, we can experience the creative and imaginative sides of ourselves.

Eloise Ristad

Indians are shy people, but we're not afraid to sing.

Bluebird Joe Parker, Salish elder

As cowboy Kenny said before performing a cappella on a stage loaded with guitarists, "My key ain't found in any of them wooden boxes." David assured me not to worry, that he'd figure out the key. All I needed to do was sing.

Before putting on the earphones, I blurted out. "I'm nervous in front of you. What will happen on stage?"

"Be brave," he replied. No one had ever said those words to me before. I tend to rush headlong into dangerous situations (which looks like bravery). The usually silent David kept talking. I can't recall his exact words but I do remember the content: his mother told him as a child that nervousness is selfish.

I felt the truth in that. Wasn't I simply worried about what others would think of me? Am I not the one who told my own kids to take leaps? To do what they wanted to do even if it might appear silly to others? I do recall my exact words: "The only one who can make a fool out of you is yourself."

And I remember my kids' response. "Sure, Mom."

I began to sing. It was like seeing myself on video for the first time—with the earphones, my own voice came back and I liked what I heard. It helped that I was singing into a microphone. With the Italian technique, you learn to get it out there with no gimmicks, just you and your breath floating on the ocean—so when you get in front of a mike the first time, it's easy. Or it seemed that way to me.

Trouble was, Patsy had deserted me. I knew the words and the tune but not the tempo. David assured me that this always happens, that the best way to learn is to listen to tapes the way I had done, then practice and practice. It's the only way, he said, to make the song your own.

It was August and hot. His pretty blond wife brought in iced tea with lemon. David and I persevered through the afternoon. He still wore the intent self-absorbed look of a pro but his face relaxed as I leaned, leaned into the song, telling the story, getting the beat, thankful for the Italian technique (you don't get tired, you just get better) and certain that God has a special place for musicians like David, willing to help a beginner get ready for the first time out.

Repetition is the key, he assured me. He never performed on his own until he got it right.

When I left the elegant bathhouse hotel that David and his wife managed, I found a small group of admirers standing outside listening. The PA system had sent me beyond the confines of the recording studio and into the parking lot. I had my first audience. Of course it didn't really count since I hadn't known they were there.

The following day at the real performance, I was nervous and began by repeating the song I had sung earlier with my teacher. The band went along with me, bands are good that way, but after the first stanza I recognized my mistake, stopped and said, "I'm singing the wrong song." The audience laughed.

It was a wonderful audience. Each person looked as if he or she would follow me anywhere. "This is my first solo," I confided and began again, nervousness forgotten. My sense of play kicked in. I didn't sound as good as the tenth time around with David the day before, but when I'd finished, I felt euphoric.

How to Focus While Performing

During my Saturday lesson after my Patsy Cline stint in Thompson Falls, my voice teacher introduced me to the art of focusing. It wasn't new, it was simply applying what I had learned from the Old Italian method. Focus involves placing the tones high and the breath low and, most important, thinking about what you are doing rather than how you are doing it. To repeat: what you are doing simply means putting the tones in the upper face—even the eyes—while breathing from the belly.

Permission. The very word relaxes a spot in my center and lets me take a deep breath. If I can permit myself to feel scared, I can also permit myself to reinterpret the scared feelings as excitement, for excitement and fear come from the same adrenaline. I can even welcome the rush from the adrenaline and know that without it my performance would be a little too relaxed and bland, a little too predictable. When I allow the adrenaline to surge, I use the energy it provides instead of fighting it. I live a little dangerously, and you in the audience pick up the excitement and bounce it right back to me. The moments when I have felt that interchange between myself and an audience have been special, and they did not come about because I managed to put a lid on my nervousness, but because I used it.

Eloise Ristad

Music being the way it is, my writing got all mixed up with ski lessons and hiking, with beekeeping and knuckle-rapping, with right brains and left brains, and a soprano on her head.

Eloise Ristad

Performance is rewarding. Still, my greatest reward in taking up singing has been an increased awareness into the workings of my own mind and heart. Once observed, such self awareness enhances confidence. Singing makes me happy.

Jo Rainbolt

"I whispered to the others that I couldn't move..they dashed about, improvising and changing the action of the scene, and singing lustily all the time. I never forgot that performance."

Homer Ulrich
quoting Lily Pons in
Famous Women Singers

Another thing I learned from my teacher that day was— don't shy away from the first note! I figured I could slide by and start on the second note, like being afraid to open the door, but when I welcomed that first note I was more focused, and it made the others more personal.

I am a natural ham, the type who plays up to an audience, and my singing skills aren't strong enough to ham and sing. By starting on the first note and continuing to focus on what I was doing (vowels and throat open? tones placed high? breath in the belly?) I was able to sing a solo at the recent funeral of my own father. My focus was so intent that I kept my eyes closed. Nobody seemed to mind.

To help overcome performance anxiety, author and pianist Eloise Ristad encourages musicians, dancers and singers to get away from their minds and into their bodies. Her book "A Soprano on Her Head" describes the methods she uses to get the inner critic out of the way.

Workshops start with freewheeling body warmups, and the soprano in the book's title somehow ended upside down on her knees. She began to sing and found all the resonance she'd been struggling for. Try it. It didn't work for the author (this is not a pretend book with a remedy-for-all) but it might work for you. To further get into the body and attune yourself ahead of time to the principles of awareness, curiosity and imagery, Ristad recommends reading "The Inner Game of Tennis" by Timothy Gallwey and "The Centered Skier" by Denise McCluggage.

Improvisation

Nicki Pisano grew up in a family where singing was as natural as eating. She didn't realize until she was an adult that not everyone sang. After performing (something she's done all her life), she'd often hear the comment "I wish I could sing." After graduating from the University of Montana with a degree in music, she started teaching nonsinging adults. "People want to sing," she said.

She still teaches private lessons but her work has led to a chanting circle. "I needed a place where I wasn't teaching and students weren't performing. We do it on a regular basis and anyone can come—it's spiritual but not religious, and it's not necessarily solemn, but joyful. I've collected chants from different cultures and groups of people."

Nicki sends out one note and everyone else responds. "We're a word oriented culture, and simple toning allows the voice to sing." From there it often turns into an experience in improvisation. "The response from each group is amazing, every single time it's a completely different experience."

Trained as a classical singer in college, Nicki felt she was missing something. So, while teaching others, she relies on the innate ability to let go and be with the breath and the body. This takes away fear and allows the freedom to improvise. Improvisation in itself is a good thing to learn since we often have to call on it when things don't go right while performing. Still, it's difficult for anyone who has had formal training, and Stephanie Judy, in her book "Making Music for the Joy of It," describes why:

In the place we call Music, improvisation is that window off to the side—an irresistible view for some musicians, all they ever look at, really. But for others, it is the Unknown...The flaw is not in ourselves but in our history. Improvisation has had a bad reputation for the last century among classical musicians and music educators, which is a shame, since it had traditionally been the backbone of a musical education. Orchestral musicians of Bach's day were often given a mere sketch of a composition, a "chart" we might call it, which they were able confidently to fill in. In recent generations, however, musical education hardened and set...classical training often inhibited the improvisation impulse by the value it placed on written music and on "being right."

I am fortunate in that my voice teacher reaches back to a

The conversational, communicative nature of improv is the heart and mettle of it— bringing smiles when you stop, and tears, too. It's in the moment, the most immediate communication possible.

Lee Zimmerman, cellist, guitarist and singer

Improvisation helps to free us in areas of our lives where we create imaginary boundaries that we dare not trespass. When I am free to improvise freely in my life, I shake hands with new parts of myself that sometimes startle, sometimes delight me. Whether startled or delighted, I always walk away more alive, more filled with me in a clean, clear way.

Eloise Ristad

Disabled folks, elders, kids, and inmates living in institutions need creative outlets. In these drab, alienating places, music raises spirits and brightens life considerably.

Folk singer/guitarist
Judith Friedman, founder of
Creativity at Any Age

At an adult day care center, a woman with acute dementia was often ignored..but she was clearly a musician. As I started to play and shape the chorus, she took hold of the hook line, singing with passion and conviction in her own style, far more in-the-groove than I was. She repeated it until we locked in together and made the song really authentic.

Judith Friedman

technique that allows for individuality. She has taught me that with the proper use of breath, I can go anywhere. This includes standing out in a thunderstorm with Liz Fee and getting a harmony to "Don't Fence Me In," something we couldn't do earlier with the proper key on the piano.

Those of us who never experienced the singing of Lily Pons still know her name. A classical singer with great verve, she became well known through records, movies and early television. Only a few people know that her nerves were so shaky during concert tours that she fought against actual illness. Still, she never stopped performing and was able to think on her feet. During a benefit performance of *The Barber of Seville* in London with the queen and king and royal family in the audience, she lost a heel from one of her slippers during the second act and, unwilling to ruin the stage picture by limping, stood in one spot for ten minutes.

You Don't Have to Leave Home to Make Music

Musicians and singers seem to operate on an intuitive level, sort of like a moccasin telegraph. No need to advertise or even fret about it, when you want to sing, it will happen.

Last October, I put together a Halloween show at the local convalescent home. Banjo-playing Matt Olason, a cowhand, 87, as old as the folks who live there, was dressed in his handmade leather mountain man outfit with a furry wolf cap. My partner Lee played the cello. I was dressed as a clown and had along some friends— six year old Ayla was a princess and Matea, five the week before, a puppy. The sunny recreation room was filled with residents and their guests, spider webs hung from the ceiling and pumpkins adorned the piano. I watched Matea crawl among the recliners and wheelchairs on all fours and go nose to nose with a child dressed as a dalmation in a red fireman's hat with a spotted body and say "I like your outfit."

The pianist didn't show up and neither did the other singers.

Matt can play and sing anything. He'd rather play his golden banjo (it really is gold), but he took over on the piano and then a woman in an orange sweatshirt decorated with falling leaves offered to play. I was still shy about singing but she was brave, and we started to sing the words to some of the old songs she knows and plays by ear. "Red River Valley." "Battle Hymn of the Republic." On that one, I felt my vowels taking over, my breath kicking in, I do love those gloooory hallehuuuulias. Ayla, Matea and I sang "Inch by inch, row by row I'm gonna make this garden grow," and other kid songs which the residents knew, too.

An old woman with a droopy lip and deformed face got up from across the room and sat down in a recliner next to me. She is developmentally disabled, and she can sing. Encouraged by her example, the pianist and I smiled at each other and sang even louder.

"You Are My Sunshine."

A favorite resident, Bertha, came in from a cigarette break and pulled me around the floor as we belted out the words to the "Tennessee Waltz."

Since that Halloween show, a few of us have met at the home each Friday at 2 p.m. The regulars include three singers (including Lee the cellist) a terrific pianist who knows all the oldies and Matt the 87-year old banjo player who devoted himself to music after retiring from the Navy over forty years ago. A friend with a lyric soprano sometimes shows up with her six-month old twins. The residents love the babies. The pianist and banjo player both had the flu last Friday and couldn't show up, but the home health nurse did. She was willing to wing it, and it turns out she has the voice and personality I've been looking for as a partner in cowgirl songs from the twenties and thirties.

Among the elders who show up to hear us sing are three silent women who love music. Their eyes light up as we sing.

We belt it out in our (Bible) church. When my daughter and I attended a Catholic memorial service, the priest commented afterwards that he'd enjoyed our singing. "I figured you girls were visitors. Catholics don't often sing like that."

Sharon Flesch,
a soprano from
Hot Springs, Montana

They sit with gracious posture and clap as if listening to a performance in a private home. One wears pearls. A fourth woman, her hands gnarled by a lifetime of hard work, wheels in with a song book in her lap and requests two favorite hymns—"Jesus Loves Me" and "Amazing Grace." The developmentally disabled woman who loves to sing joined in louder than ever when I sang the Norwegian prayer that I sang at my father's funeral. The nurse told me they knew nothing of the woman's background and wondered if she could have heard the language as a child. (I didn't, and Matt the old banjo-playing Norske who'd transcribed the song from English says I have a "unique accent.")

It's freeing to learn a song in another language. Look for a native speaker and practice speaking the words. I don't learn languages easily and have no intention of mastering Italian but when I first started voice lessons I read Italian aloud to Rosa Caselli, a native Italian speaker who owned a restaurant in California and has retired to Hot Springs. The reading helped open up my troublesome vowel sounds. Nothing beats hands-on practice. Rosa's son taped Italian conversation from TV shows, and I'd listen while working around the house.

When you acquire a new passion such as singing (or finally indulge yourself after years of wishing to sing), you'll find all sorts of people who share it. Step outside the boundaries of your job or neighborhood. If you live in a city, all the opportunities are already there, everything from barbershop to rap to chanting. Such groups are always willing to include new members and, trust me, it's better therapy than most counseling. If you live in a small town, it's easy to create situations.

Every town has a nursing home with a recreation room and a piano. Churches are good places to sing. This past Christmas, four of us got together weekly for a month and practiced a four-part harmony to "Ave Maria" which we sang in three different churches. Regardless of our beliefs, Christmas and Easter music bring out the singer in all of us.

Each week we would close the session with a raucous sing-along of mostly folk songs..new to the majority of the residents and required honest-to-God effort, but no one seemed to mind. 'Blowing in the Wind' received the same vigorous interpretation as 'Hava Nagilah.' My elderly friends learned lyric after lyric, chorus upon verse. Use it or lose it, studies tell us. 'Studies, shmuddies,' my friends might have said, 'let's just have fun.'

Jessica Baron Turner,
educator and author

Singers are everywhere. While singing Christmas carols with a large appreciative audience in the old hotel that serves as a social center, my attention was drawn to a young lady standing in the back of the room. She sang with her shoulders back and her dark eyes wide-open. Dressed in black with her long hair draped around her face, she could have been a teenage opera singer from the earlier era of singers I admire so much. I motioned her to come join the group of "singers" grouped around the piano (I emphasize singers because there were plenty of shy ones singing in the crowd), and she came at once, singing her way through the crowd. During a break, she took my compliments in stride and told me she's fourteen and a mezzo soprano. I wouldn't have been surprised to hear her burst into an Italian aria. She'd just moved to town with her father and lived in one of the cramped apartments behind the hotel.

When you sense your talent is genuinely wanted and needed somewhere and you like the people, it's time to give it a try. In the end, you may come to agree that there's no better soul food than being of service.

Jessica Baron Turner

Singing in School

Small schools seem to attract teachers gifted in the art of creating something from nothing. Having lived most of my life in rural communities, I've witnessed time and again the amazing results of making do. Hot Springs is not a town of means (seventy five percent of the six hundred residents live at or below the poverty level), but a recent performance of "Aladdin's Lamp" directed by music, band and drama teacher Susan Kretschmar demonstrated what ingenuity can do.

She had no budget to work with, yet the old stucco gymnasium was transformed into a magical kingdom. The front hall (where popcorn and basketball tickets are usually sold) became a dimly-lit alleyway leading into the city of Baghdad. A veiled beauty sold tickets from behind a small window cut into the brick wall. Inside the gym, giant palm trees and camels were but a few of the props that carried the audience into the land of Aladdin. The seating was inventive—blocks of diagonal rows with an aisle down the center where some of the action took place. The entire gym with its varnished walls and floors was put to good use: a market place on one end (food, drinks, goods and face-painting were sold before and after the play) with the stage acting as a castle. Action wasn't confined to the downstairs—the play started out by spot lighting an evil queen and her equally evil brother in the upper balcony that surrounds the gym. Some members of the audience had to crane their necks in order to see, but action also took place in the opposite balcony, including a huge paper-mache rock which was heaved from it by Aladdin.

The energy from the players, unusual seating, lighting, props and lavish costumes kept my attention from the moment I entered the enchanted alleyway. The play was a huge success, a romp. A measure of its success was the way it was received by kids and adults. Grade schoolers who saw it earlier in the day urged everyone in town to go to the evening performance. Later, talking to Susan Kretschmar, I realized the genius behind the production.

Two-inch PVC pipe, chicken wire, cardboard and butcher paper were the main materials for the big props such as camels, walls and palm trees. Susan said anyone on a tight budget should look at prom decoration books for backdrop ideas, then make the stuff yourself rather than purchasing it. She said this was the first musical done in Hot Springs and that, although the students had picked Aladdin, the old fear of singing in public set in when word got out that it was a musical and not just a play. Rumors flew, it looked as if most of the kids weren't going to audition; so Susan met with her drama club and got the word out that few of the players would solo, and that songs could be recited if needed. Forty five kids from grades seven through twelve auditioned (there are only a hundred kids in the high school), and there were parts for everyone, on stage or off. A local collector of vintage clothing hit the thrift shops, and (with the help of high school girls that she paid), sewed up the wonderfully bangled, spangled costumes for free.

During the spring concert for the elementary school, Susan

once again demonstrated her ingenuity. "I'm easily bored," she explained, "so I look for ways to keep others interested." The program featured "goofy" songs—work, play and family folk songs with an unusual twist that kept our ancestors going through good and hard times, and to erase any doubts that such singing was simply for play, she reeled off an impromptu list of benefits—from enhancing memorization skills to learning pronunciation, history and vocabulary.

Some of the songs required audience participation, others featured verses made up by the students. During the final "Swing Low Sweet Chariot" number, all the grades from kindergarten through sixth surrounded the audience and sang the song in rounds. "Being in the middle of a circle of singing children gave me a sense of community," one mother commented after the concert, "we were changed from individuals to being a part of it."

Community Theaters

A small town is what a city neighborhood used to be. We have everything we need. Except for browsing at the university library, I didn't have to leave home in order to write this book. Whenever a problem came up, the solution followed. I met Liz Fee, a retired journalist and singer, at the local library. I call her with questions ranging from "how much voice technique does the reader need?" to "what makes a pop song popular?"

Liz and I went to Plains twenty miles away to attend a production of *The Sound of Music*. When the seven von Trapp children began to sing "Doe a Deer, A Female Deer," it was obvious they'd been trained to sing, and when Mother Superior sang her first solo, it was a good guess that she'd coached them. During intermission, I found out that Mother Superior is Jan Olson in real life, a minister's wife as active in church, school and community singing as she was during her years as a public school music teacher.

I play the flute and read music and I've always said that I couldn't sing without seeing the notes. But harmony is something else. You have to hear it. We have three church services and sing four new songs a Sunday, with no rehearsals, and I had to take a leap in order to sing harmony. I prayed for it.

Debra Martell,
the author's niece from
Hartford, Wisconsin

My college roommate and I were both shy. Since we intended to teach, we figured we'd better get over it, so we enrolled in voice lessons.

Retired music teacher
Jan Olson

85

Later, talking to Jan, she resisted that word "coach"—"encourage" is more in keeping with her character. In fact, she said encouragement is all it takes to get a community theater going in a small town, even with a major production such as *The Sound of Music.* "Somebody always has a bee in their bonnet and gets things started. Piano was my major in music school, along with flute, and I enjoy accompanying."

"We had to help each other extra hard (in *The Sound of Music*) because most of us were sick. We all encouraged each other to reach those high notes."

A sense of sharing is essential. Projects are undermined when one well-meaning but overzealous person attempts to do everything. Responsibility only stretches so far. Burn out is inevitable, and so is grumbling among the ranks. "Be flexible," Jan said, "Let the leadership change. Once a town gets a theater or musical group going, somebody's energy keeps it going."

She suggested doing musical projects with a goal in mind. "Do short term commitments. I just worked with a men's group. We met for four to six weeks just to sing, and on a Sunday morning hit four churches. When getting a group together, you're going to hear 'I like to sing, but I can't read notes.' It doesn't matter if they sing by rote or by notes. It sounds good, everybody gets a feeling of accomplishment."

But if you want to bite off a big chunk and stage a musical, do it. Jan says the leads will show up along with somebody crazy about piano, and another person into period costume design. "Go to the schools," she said "and get the kids involved; do some educating at the same time. Anything with a passion involved generates enthusiasm. Share that enthusiasm and it multiplies."

While interviewing people over eighty for a newspaper column, I found that it's enthusiasm—not lifestyle or diet or beliefs—that keeps humans vital into old age. Jan wasn't surprised when she heard this. "If you trace the word to the Latin, it means being with God."

Happy singing journey. May enthusiasm light your way.

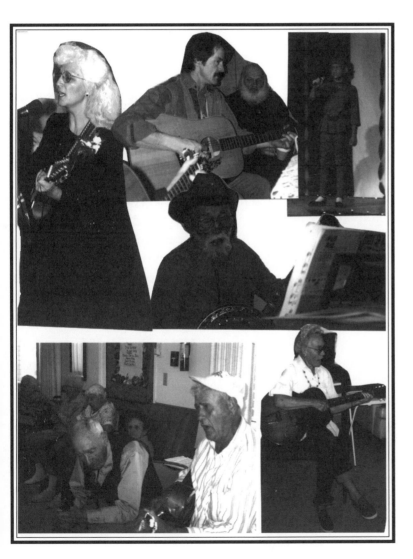

Singers from Hot Springs, Montana

Clockwise—Faith Chosa (photo by Gale Watson); Wes Huffman on banjo with Paul Mahoney singing; Brittney Graham, Junior Miss 1997; Theresa Collum yodeling for residents at the convalescent home; Lyle Hosterman and Tom Stanford at the home. Center photo is Matt Olason at Cowboy Fred's memorial service.(Photos by Jo Rainbolt).

PART TWO

Vocal Technique

Voice teacher and author Bonnie Jean Triplett in performance with her voice teacher Maestro Robert Knowles, Denver, Colorado, 1975.
                    Photo by Barbara Barnwell

Chapter 5
Using the Breath

"When we have mastered the internal word, when we have vividly and clearly conceived a figure or a statue, when we have found a musical theme, expression is complete, nothing more is needed. If, then, we open our mouth, and speak or sing.... what we do is to sing aloud what we have already sung within." Philosopher Benedetto Croce.

"The breath is the ocean; the voice is the boat which floats on the ocean." Singing voice teacher Giovanni Battista Lamperti.

The old Italian master method of vocal technique is the most recognized and durable. Regardless of the musical style that you have chosen to sing, it requires this method of artistic execution.

Breath is your friend, make your breath your constant companion.

To begin, you will learn how to use the breath. Stand straight and tall with good posture. The head is up and relaxed. Breathe deeply and slowly exhale. Learn to control the breathing very low in the abdomen. Fill the lungs abundantly with air, though quietly and without haste. The lower abdomen should inflate like a balloon. This deep breathing should make you feel very hollow in the head, neck and chest down to the waistline. You need to satisfy the lungs without dissipating the hollow feeling of the upper torso. The top and the bottom of the lungs should be equally full of air.

A singer must cultivate the power to quickly draw in a full breath, and exhale it out so gradually that one can sing a musical phrase lasting ten to fifteen seconds, sometimes up to twenty seconds. A singer's respiration is a considerable amplification of the ordinary breathing... inspiration and expiration. For singing purposes, diaphramatic breathing must be combined with rib breathing.[1]

Singers should fill their lungs while keeping their throats loose and wide open, and without raising the upper part of the chest, as they strive for noiseless and imperceptible breathing. They should have some breath in reserve at the end of singing a musical phrase.

Relax the mouth when you are singing. The mouth is an opening for the breath only. The actual work of singing is done in the remainder of the body. Your tongue should lie flat, relaxed and perfectly quiet in your mouth, not flexed or tense. To obtain this feeling of a "relaxed, open throat," start with a big yawn. Notice the opening of the mandibular joint at the back of your mouth. Now close your mouth somewhat keeping the teeth open at the back of your mouth-- still retaining the opening at the back of the mouth with a feeling as though the jaw is unhinged. Your cheeks should be raised. If you looked in the mirror you would see that your mouth is now opened to about the width of your finger. That small opening of the teeth in front is wide enough to take in the breath needed to sing.

Now try the deep breathing. Take in a deep breath, feeling the lower abdomen inflating like a balloon. Breathe deeply and noiselessly. Exhale slowly. Let the air flow out gently and very gradually, under complete control. Breathe deeply once again. To start your musical tone, release the breath fusing the voice and the breath. Use an "ah" sound on any pitch.

The energized breath is controlled by your diaphragm. Your breath should come as a sigh. Lean on the breath deep into your pelvis. Leaning into the breath, for you as a singer, is like preparing your abdomen to work, as you would when you were preparing to lift something heavy. Then let your voice go of its own weight. Breath is the impulse for the singing voice. Energized air, the escaping breath, feeds the pulsation in the vocal cords of your throat. The energy of musical tone and the energy of breath must be in balance. The air should be equally distributed among all of the tones to be sung in one breath, and it should flow quietly and noiselessly.

For first time singers, try singing musical tones on a vowel sound of "ah" on a diatonic scale in the key of C Major. If it is needed, there are books available to teach musical notation. One of them is <u>The Basic Guide To How To Read Music</u> by Helen Cooper, by The Berkley Publishing Group.

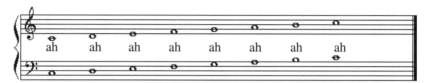

Then try another exercise. Using the same vowel sound "ah", try the chromatic scale.

When you are comfortable with those musical tones, try singing intervals: Major Second; Major Third; Perfect Fourth; Perfect Fifth; Major Sixth; Major Seventh; and Octaves. Sing them first with the vowel sound of "ah." Then sing them with other vowel sounds.

Now as you are learning about the use of the breath, try one other vocal exercise. Sing with the vowel sound "ah" the Major Triad that has within it the Major Third and the Perfect Fifth.

Breath gives us wings. Even for birds, flying is riding the air current, the breath, under the wings. Allow the singer proper breath energy, and the singer gives wings to the voice.

Chapter 6

Legato

In Italian "legato" means bound together. A singer's voice moves smoothly from one tone into another tone. The breath may not be interrupted between the first tone and the next tone, but must be held as though they are one.

By proper use of the singer's breath, "there can be inside the body an opposition between the muscles which send out the breath and the muscles which draw in the breath. A singer can press out and hold back in such a way what when he sings, he need not contact the throat."[1]

As you are learning, feel yourself sing. Don't listen to yourself sing.

Your larynx, that is the upper part of the windpipe or trachea, should remain quiet through a song. A quiet throat is the result of the interrelation of vocal energy and breath power. The relationship between voice vibration and breath is like the relation between the string vibration and the bow of a violin. Quietly inhaled breath must be drawn out, not pushed out. The singing voice comes from the overtones of regular vibrations of the vocal cords. When a tone is pure, then the lower, harmonious overtones are the only ones that are heard in the singing voice. If a voice is forced, then the higher and discordant harmonics predominate, which causes a hard, metallic, and sharp quality to the human voice.

Singers transform each air wave into a tone wave. The tone wave must pass out freely and unhindered. It is directed against the front part of the roof of the mouth. A good tone is one that is true, bright and free. The voice moves from one note to another as the will directs. The notes seem to join, yet they are "clean cut pearls on a string." [1]

Of the old Italian masters, "Crescentini affirmed that the art of singing is looseness of the neck and voice above the breath; neither the neck nor any part of it, the throat, the tongue or the jaw, should be rigid when the voice is produced, and the breath should be regulated by the muscles inside the body under the larynx, so that the note can be felt, as it were, resting on it. The looseness of the (vocal) instrument must be such as to give rise to the sensation of the note resting on the breath."[2] The old masters saw the blending of the notes without a slip or a slur as equally important as producing of a note with a clear and bright tone.

Start the singing tone as a musician starts the tone of a violin. Once again use vocal exercises. Starting your musical tones-- release the energized breath fusing the voice with the breath. As you move to the different tones, connect one tone with another.

Try this vocal exercise using the same vowel sound "ah." If it is needed, there are some books into print that teach about musical notation. Among those, there is one that I have come to appreciate. It is The Basic Guide To How To Read Music by Helen Cooper. Published by The Berkley Publishing Group.

Now try the vocal exercise with an additional note added...

In trying this exercise, observe that you are connecting the tones without any interruption of the breath. A tone must be self-starting, self-prolonging, and self-stopping. To make this possible complete management of breathing is a necessity. Singing depends upon a sense of hearing. The physical ear perceives and knows how a pure tone is to sound in a voice and in musical instruments. The mental ear perceives little by little how to produce this pure sound. Singing is instinctive, but its control is subconscious.

Chapter 7
Focus of Singing Tones

Singing has two extremes -- the depth of the abdomen and the height of the placement in the skull, the nasal placement. Use a high nasality to locate the correct placement. You should sing above the soft palate, that is, above the roof or upper part of the mouth. Every syllable sung is directed into the nasal cavity. The focal point of the musical tone is in the head.

Imagery helps the beginning singer to focus tones. The singer needs an "open throat." Feel the expansion in your throat when you attempt to swallow; the peak of the swallow motion is the openness the singer desires. It lowers the larynx. Another source of imagery is the motion of the yawn; the feeling of expansion in the throat at the initiation of a yawn also produces the desired openness of the throat. Another way to express it is to open the mouth horizontally rather than vertically.

Form the words of a song with the tip of the tongue and the front of the teeth. Raise your mouth so high that only the tip of the tongue can barely form the words. Stay focused in the facial mask. Try correctly pronouncing the word "England" slowly. When you sense the vibration of the "ng" in the word "England" you have found the spot where a singing tone should start.

Remember, the mouth should be relaxed when you are singing. The mouth is only an opening for the breath. The cheeks should be raised. The tongue should lie quietly extended in the mouth; it is not raised in the center nor drawn back. The jaw is unconstrained, balanced and feels as though it is floating. The lower jaw is independent of movements of the tongue. Meribeth Bunch has said, "the most favorable conditions of the pharynx (the muscular sac which intervenes between the cavity of the mouth and the esophagus, whose contraction aids in the swallowing of food,) to attain vocal quality are an elevated soft

The focal point of the musical tone is in the head.

palate, comfortably low larynx, a relaxed tongue, and a lack of tension in the neck and back."[1]

Try another vocal exercise. To start your musical tones, release the energized breath by fusing the voice and the breath. You should be releasing energy in regular vibrations, and you should feel that vibration focused in the middle of the skull. You will learn that it is not the amount of the breath that matters in your singing, but rather the direction in which you place that breath. You are directing or focusing that breath as high as possible in the facial mask. The sensation of resonance is ever present. In this exercise sing the sound "nee" that is a long vowel sound of "e", and then the sound "ah" in this fashion...

Use a high nasality to find the correct placement; focus your breath as high as possible in the facial mask.

Starting on the Perfect 5th, that is a note of G in a C Major scale, and move down the notes of a diatonic scale to the root of C in this way--

Nee-ee-ee-ee-ah-ah-ah.

Try the vocal exercise some more in other keys by moving up and down the Major scale.

Your voice will stay focused in the skull as long as you sing with regular vibration in the throat that is fed by energized breath controlled in the pelvis/abdomen. The more sensation of resonance in your head cavities, the better placement of your voice. Musical tones form and exist above the palate regardless of the pitch. Your voice is focused sufficiently when all of the tones in your range are intense enough to feel as though they are started and stopped in the same spot-- that is the spot in the center of the skull.

Experiment with another vocal exercise. This is an arpeggio, a broken chord with notes played in succession. Use the syllables "Na" with a long vowel sound on the "a", and "No" with a long vowel sound on the "o." Use those sounds in this pattern--

Na-No-Na-No-Na-No-Na-No-Na.

100

Start out this exercise in the key of C Major. Then try the same exercise in other keys by moving up and down the Major scale.

Chapter 8
Diction, Pronunciation, Articulation

In the language which is the word of song, diction has taken on its own meaning. The primary definition of diction concerns the choice of words: the clearness or effectiveness of wording, written or spoken, and secondarily the distinctness of speech. The singer's definition is pronunciation and enunciation of words in singing.[1]

Diction embraces pronunciation, enunciation and articulation, three terms which have grown fuzzy in recent useage and now tend to be interchangeable. Articulate means to pronounce distinctly and carefully; to enunciate. Articulation refers more specifically to the adjustment and movement of speech organs: the tongue, the lips and the teeth involved in the formation of sound, especially a consonant.[2] Enunciation emphasizes clarity in pronouncing words resulting in ease of perception by the listener. Pronunciation is a comprehensive definition: the act or result of producing the sounds of speech, including articulation, vowel formation, accent, inflection and intonation, often with reference to the correctness or acceptability of speech sounds. (American College Dictionary, Random House, 1966)

Pronunciation is usually the biggest handicap for American singers who are enculturated with faulty speech. To correctly pronounce your words in singing use only the tip of the tongue and the front of the teeth. Never separate pronunciation from singing, not even in thought. Lyric linkage of sounds, the syllables and the words is necessary in the flow of a song.[3] In this singing use, linkage means the manner or style of being fitted together or united. This leads to the "legato" essential to singing in any language. Dorothy Uris has written, "the main vehicle of linkage-

Singing is speaking in musical tones.

legato is the sustained and recognizable vowel. A consonant, whether printed as part of the previous word, or the next word, leads syllables in the forward drive of word rhythms. No English vowel or consonant need interrupt the momentum of the phrase; English does not cut the vocal flow, singers do. The practice of seeing and feeling connected sounds in advance reinforces legato singing."[4]

Singing is sustained speech. Author Russell Hammar says, "singing is an extension of speech. Every vowel has its unique size and shape on every given pitch and dynamic level. An excellent singing practice is to carefully pronounce a word that is to be sung. There must be enough lift of the soft palate, or slight yawning, to add to the depth of the tone. However, the addition of depth must always be within the confines of the correct vowel focus."[5]

The clearly defined "ah" vowel sound should be in the singer's mind with forward focus behind the upper front teeth.[6]

Consonants move laterally. They do not move up or down. Your speech is located in one, high-placed position. It is that high, nasal placement that we have talked about in the earlier chapter. What you need to be alert to is the tendency to use the mouth too much, to use your lips too much, in forming the words when you are singing. That tendency is strong when singing lyrics in the American language. Raise your mouth so high that only the tip of the tongue can barely form the words. "The singer must form the vowel in proper size and shape subconsciously before he begins to produce the tone which is to be sung," says Hammar.[7] "Consonants must not interfere with the basic resonance, breath action and vowel formations for singing."[8]

Try an exercise that helps you to find some comfort and ease with a high-placed, nasal sound. One hint, when singing an "ah" sound, be certain that it is placed and sounds like the "ah" in the English word "apple" with an additional thrust of nasality. For the beginning singer, a vowel spectrum exercise would include these sounds:

long E vowel, such as in the word "feel";

long A vowel, such as in the word "bay";

short vowel sound of Ah, as in the word "animal";

long O vowel sound, as in the word "note";

short O vowel sound, as in the word "shoe";

A much broader listing of vowel sounds and other sounds is to be found in the Chapter 13 of this book in further study in pronunciation in English.

For your first exercise use the following consonants and vowels:

May-ay-ay-ay-Moh-oh-oh-oh-Mah-ah-ah-ah-ah-ah-ah-ah-ah.

Try the vocal exercise in other keys that move up and down the Major scale.

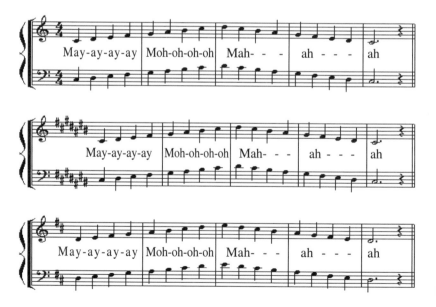

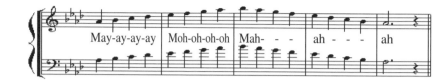

May-ay-ay-ay   Moh-oh-oh-oh   Mah- - -   ah - - -   ah

The body must be developed and organized in order to produce the unseen and unfelt energy that serves the sound of the words and pitch of the tones. Find a symbol, an image, or a thought, that will lead and unify all efforts. A constant bouyancy in the head, in the neck and in the upper chest is essential to free tone production and good pronunciation. Author Hammar says, "One should approach the singing in all languages by employing clear, simple vowel sounds with a 'softening' of plosive consonants. Vowels in singing should be pure and precise; the consonants should be elegant and free from constriction."[9]

If it is possible for you to do so, learn to sing in and correctly pronounce the words of the Italian language and the German language. "In Italian the vowels are prolonged and the consonants are rapidly passed over, whereas the characteristics of the English language is to pass rapidly from the vowels to the consonants," says Shakespeare. [10] When singing in the English language then, practice saying outloud the lyrics of the song before singing the lyrics of the song. In this way you can check yourself with the sound of the words to ensure that you are pronouncing them with a raised speech.

Rosa Ponselle, American Soprano

Chapter 9
Fusing the Voice and the Breath

Balance breath and musical tone.

The two extremes that you use in singing are: the height of the nasal placement and the depth of the breath. The production of a singing tone is dependent on the sustained intensity of initial vibration and the continuous release of inherent breath energy. "The larynx containing the vibrating instrument must be placed or balanced in the right position over the breath. If after a noiseless breath, we start the note in the very center of the pitch, purity of the vowel is the result, the placing muscles act, and the note responds to a pressure which we must learn to balance and economize, as though warming some object."[1]

When your singing voice becomes a reality it will use all of the energies of your mind and body as easily as the speaking voice does. Every note should be energized. The difference between speaking and singing is the continuity of vibration and energy: in speaking the momentum is constantly arrested; in singing the continuity is never arrested.

Hahn has commented, "Many singers make no distinction between supporting and pushing (of the breath). These are two different things. What is support? Support is distinct contact between breath and tone, which may be pronounced or barely perceptible but is always exact and firm."[2]

If your voice cracks, your breath is not fused to your voice. Steady voice is steady breath.

Maximize the feeling of singing with imagery. Feel as though the breath is taken into a place that is located in the sternum in the chest, imagine that it is an opening in the middle of your body. When the breath is taken into this opening direct it downward. "Lean" on the breath when you sing as though you were preparing the abdomen to lift something heavy. Feel a lateral spread at the back of the mouth. Pretend that the area of the body in which you are breathing and singing is located in the center and is like a tube. Then pull the breath through it like you are pulling a rope through the tube-- a big tube and a rope that has knots. The knots are the consonants that you are singing. Prepare to sing each succeeding phrase while you are still singing the one preceding it. Learn to stay steady on the breath.

All sounds form and exist above the palate regardless of pitch of the music. A singer only allows the sound to change pitch, nothing else changes. The sounds form and stay working in the same area; you do not go up or down. Russell Hammar says, "the singer must simultaneously imagine both the pitch and the tone color of what he is speaking on the vocal pitches in order to give adequate expression to the music and vocal efforts," and he says, "the placement of vowel focus should always be felt behind the front teeth -- in the forward section of the hard palate; yet with enough arching of the soft palate to give depth to the tone."[3] To learn this sensation pretend that there is an imaginary, horizontal line between the cheek bones in the face. Now think of singing on the level of that imaginary line.

Reynaldo Hahn said, "the real beauty and value of singing is the combination, the mixing, of the indissoluble union of sound and thought."[4]

Human voices can be recognized as having three registers: the chest register; the medium register; and the head register. The Italian word "passagio" refers to a point in voice register transition, or a passage, from one register to another. "There may be three registers, but when rightly produced, these so dovetail, as it were, one into the other, as to form one long even voice."[5] Meribeth Bunch says, "A good teacher can correct the adjusting for registers by showing the singer how to bridge the gaps in his transitions of registers, thus giving the impression of a single register with notes of equal quality but differing pitch."[6]

Energy in regular vibrations is constructive. Regular vibration makes the voice feel like one register. It makes it feel

It is not the amount of breath that matters in singing, but rather the direction in which you place that breath.

like one mechanism from top to bottom. The head and the pelvis are mysteriously connected by the coordination of all of the activities that lie between them. Meribeth Bunch says, "a singer should begin a sound with prior thought and a proper attack, and at the same time be able to maintain a tone of constant loudness and pitch. This constancy of tone requires a constant pressure just below the vocal folds, the subglottic pressure."[7] The singer catches the next tone mentally before the one that he or she is singing stops spinning.

In singing various tones within a voice register, a singer who is moving from the low-pitched tones to the high-pitched tones must take the opposite direction with the breath from the tone of the voice. The higher the pitch of the tone the lower in the abdomen that the singer feels for it; the lower the pitch of the tone the higher in the abdomen the singer feels for it. He or she is always leaning on the breath deep into the pelvis and focusing that tone high in the facial mask, doing all of the work on the inside with no exterior movements. The exciting of the muscular energy prepares the singer to sing. The memory of how it feels to sing makes his or her only method.

Try another vocal exercise. In this exercise use the consonants-

-

Nee-ee-ee-No-o-o-Nah-ah-ah-ah--

Start this exercise in the key of C Major. The beginning note is an octave above middle C.

At another time when you practice this exercise, change the consonants to sing--

Lee-ee-ee-Lo-o-o-Lah-ah-ah-ah.

Chapter 10

Summation—
Word, Tone and Breath

Do not listen to yourself sing. Feel yourself sing.

Openness of the throat gives the sensation of air coming in when you are singing rather than the feeling of air going out.

"Settle down" on your breath while singing. Find the lowest possible place in the abdomen in which you breathe and in which you sing. Keep leaning; always moving in the directions of "down and out."

"The higher the note in any register, the greater is the pressure of breath required, and the greater the art in controlling this pressure. On the other hand, the lower the note, the feebler is the sound, by reason of the comparative slackness of the vocal cords. The singer's skill is displayed scarcely less in intensifying this low sound without losing command of the breath. The vocal cords under such conditions are poised and balanced, as it were, on the breath. The fullest tone is produced with the least breath."[1]

Raise the roof of your mouth so high that the tongue can barely form the words.

An unimpeded path for the breath is desired while singing. The tones begin very low in the abdomen. The resonances are formed very high in the head. These directions, both up and down, are found quickly and readily by an accomplished singer; a skill that is expressed with an ease that equals or exceeds their use of spoken language.

"Freedom of the jaw can be recognized by the unconscious ease with which the tongue can assume not only the different positions necessary for the vowel sounds, but can execute also the movements for the tongue consonants of l,d,t,n,and r, and the hard consonants of g,k and th, without the slightest movement of the jaw. On freedom of the jaw depends the freedom of the larynx. Freedom of the lips is of great importance as a sign of singing rightly. The upper lip shall be raised as in smiling."[2]

For correct placement, "lean" into the nasal cavities as if there existed two points of prongs holding the upper mouth high and open. Use pure vowel sounds when forming your tones. Approach your consonants laterally. The back of the mouth opens in a horizontal manner.

The enormous vocal power of a singer comes from the energized breath. It is obtained by slowly and silently inhaling air until the body has air from the pelvis to the collar bone with little or no expansion of the upper lungs. The singer's control of this enormous power is evidenced by the ease with which tones are started and sustained, and the distinctness of pronunciation.

The voice needs regular vibration and full resonance for it to be controlled. This is what a natural singer does with his or her voice. The throat feels "open" only when pronunciation controls the vibration, resonance, and breath energy as a unit. There needs to be a perfect attack at the start of the tone as the singer begins a musical phrase. Another way of viewing voice production is: "on the basis of the right breath control, the vocal instrument can be tuned in unconscious freedom, and the tongue can assume any position necessary to pronunciation. Consequently, the space at the back of the tongue, as well as the cavity of the mouth, is now completely under control, and the tone demands a certain open state of throat; he who knows how to pronounce, and (how to) control the breath, knows how to sing. A perfect freedom of throat and tongue enables us to adjust the tone-space by the same act as that which we pronounce. The quiescent and entirely unrestrained condition of the back of the throat, in the instant before drinking, is that which should accompany every note that we sing."[3]

The breath is the impulse for the singing. Singing is knowing mentally what you have to do physically to control the breath.

The mouth is only an opening for the breath. The singing is done in the rest of the body.

Release your breath slowly, fusing the voice and breath.

Unite the breath with the tones. Regular vibration causes the voice to be true in pitch, ringing in quality, and rich in character. It demands breath controlled by the diaphragm.

Because inherent energy in air secures both the pitch of tones and the power of tones, the singer feels the control of the breath descend in the pelvis of the body as the voice ascends the scale or increases in volume. The carrying power of the human singing voice depends upon the regularity and intensity of vibration of the breath energy.

The singing voice must have an inexhaustible supply of both regular vibration and breath power for each musical phrase.

When your tone emerges from silence into sound without effort, focused yet free, and the tone emerges with sufficient breath energy to release it or restrain it, then you are a singer. To sing well you must continually feel "hollow-headed, full-throated, broad-chested, and tight-waisted," says Giovanni Battista Lamperti. Do not hold your tones, but spin them. Instead of holding your tones, hold your breath. Do not dissipate the hollow feeling in your body, but rather breathe through it.

The singer is in command of every note; the technique is not just executed but polished.

Singing is a balance of contending forces. Your voice is focused sufficiently when all of the tones in your range are intense enough to feel as though they are started and stopped in the same spot-- that is in the center of the skull. When you can start your voice with your mouth closed as well as when your mouth is open, then you are focused to sing. A focused tone is a self-starting, self-stopping sound: effortless, nonviolent, and yet intense vibrations of the vocal cords cause the tones to focus.

Feel as though your musical notes are resting on your breath.

"The artist can increase the intensity of his tone without increasing its volume, and thus can produce the softest effects in the largest theaters. By his skill he can cause this soft note to be heard as far as a loud one, arousing feelings-- as of distance, and such emotions as memories of the past may bring. He can produce equally well the more powerful gradations, until he reaches fortissimo, without overstepping that control which is the boundary of noble and expressive singing."[4]

Voice master Francesco Lamperti taught, "never sing with more voice than that which you can produce when you rightly control the breath. The force of the voice should always be less than the force of the breath that supports it. The voice should be dominated by the breath, and not the breath by the voice."

Bazzini, an Italian musician said, "the end of art is not to astonish, but to move."

"Bel Canto" singing was, "... concerned with perfecting the lightness and flexibility of the voice, and the delivery of the melodic phrase. Its aim was an infinitely varied tone quality, an impeccable purity of pronunciation, everything possible in terms of sonority, and purely physical realization of sound. What was particularly sought after in Bel Canto was a certain tonal quality: a smoothness and flexibility of sound, the ability to produce many sonorities." (clear, loud, full-volumed sound)[5]

Singing is a balance act, like a circus tight rope act.

Progression in singing is refining the line that you are singing on until you are completely independent of it. When you are singing correctly your tones are floating-- like a balance of movements. When you have correctly engaged the vocal technique, the breath control feels as though you can turn on a thin dime as you change the musical notes and move through a melody.

To the many students of singing who have read through the words of imagery in this book, try to follow instructions given. Be patient with yourself when you are first learning how to sing. It takes practice to learn how to coordinate these mental and physical processes.

Set modest goals for yourself allowing sufficient time to learn. Aim for the level of complexity of music that you want to sing as a competent singer. Make it a personal decision of a goal, not a proficiency defined by others. Select vocal music that gradually brings you to your goal-defined level of performance. The voice, as a musical instrument, builds its strength by starting to sing music which is simple in structure; then moving forward to music which is more complex. Select appropriate choices of vocal music that follow that principle. Sing the music you like, and you will like the music you sing.

Enrico Caruso as Canio in Leoncavallo's
I Pagliacci

Chapter 11

Problem Solving in Vocal Technique

The most frequent problems are singing with loose breath or singing with gutteral tones. Diffused sounds, that is the lack of focus of vowel sounds, produce weak or breathy tones because of wasted breath.

Muscular tension is the main cause of a bad tone. Muscular tension results from undue pressure or restraint of the tone. The tongue under tension can thicken and draw back partly closing the throat. The jaw becomes set and stiff.

When you are having difficulties with singing return to the basics-- a sigh and a cry. Start the singing tone on a sigh, and focus the tone in a nasal placement as in a cry. A singer's bad habits are merely efforts of protection against clumsy management of the breath. A glottal stroke, which is an explosion of the tone at the beginning of a phrase, can be corrected by "sighing" into the tone. If the voice cracks on a high tone, it is because you are opening your mouth too much, and the tongue rises creating tension. The breath helps the throat to open.

Never strain to reach a note. For high tones try to be so far above them that you are "looking down" on the tones. For low tones, place them high in your mouth.

To start correcting your singing, check to feel if you are breathing properly. Review the chapter on instructions for breathing. Follow the steps through so that they can become a check list as you make amendments.

If pronouncing words "closes" the throat, then you are not using the breath correctly. If the high tones are pinched and small, you do not have adequate breath support. Neither can the singer be "pushing" too much on the breath or forcing the tone. The breath must come like a sigh; it is leaning on the tone.

As the voice ascends to higher tones, the control of the breath descends deeper into the abdomen or pelvis. On low tones, control is felt at the diaphragm and even higher. When breath is held and controlled in the abdomen, then the voice is free to expand to any tone whether it be a high or a low tone. It is not the amount of breath that matters, but rather the direction that the singer gives to the breath.

The average vibrato of the human voice is five to eight regular pulsations per second. Meribeth Bunch says, "pulsations slower than five per second are easily picked up by the human ear as separate pitches, and are unpleasant. This excessively slow vibrato is often referred to as a wobble and can be caused by muscle fatigue, emotional tension, or excessive contraction of intrinsic muscles of the larynx. A rate of much more than eight pulsations per second is normally too fast and produces either an unpleasant sound like a bleat or a tremolo, and is often caused by too much pressure on the focal folds."[1]

If, having reviewed the chapter on breath control, you discover that you are controlling your breath correctly, but are still having difficulties, then feel for these other possibilities of deficiencies in voice production.

Are you focusing the tones correctly? Are your tones too far forward in the mouth, or too far back in the pharynx? Resonance is in the middle of the skull. Place the tones very high in the facial mask. The place in which you should be singing is a place so high in nasality that it seems as though you cannot reach it. A description that Jo uses in her singing of low tones is to "place it high and sing it low." Those two thoughts reach the desired results for her.

Other than incorrect breath control, the second most frequent problem is incorrect pronunciation. Russell Hammar reminds the singers, "malformation of the vowel leads to muscular tension (and vice versa), and this distortion of the resonator is the central cause of the singer's poor tone production."[2]

Vocal warm-up exercises remind your body that it is time to work; it is a physical activity for the breath more than for the voice.

If pronunciation is correct and tones are placed high, you can go anywhere, as long as you remember to go with the breath.

Reynaldo Hahn said, "Frequently it is preoccupation with the beauty and roundness of the sound that causes singers to pronounce badly. If words cannot be understood it is usually due to a distorted vowel, though occasionally, it is due to weak consonants. It is difficult to maintain perfect evenness while at the same time paying attention to the exact mouth position required by the vowels. In singing, it is not necessary to move the lips grotesquely in order to pronounce well."[3]

Practice outloud saying the lyrics of the music to listen for incorrect pronunciation of words. Recall that a singer uses European raised speech. All that you need of mouth movement in order to form words is the tip of the tongue and the front of the teeth in English. Place the syllables in the nose. Practice saying the words of the lyrics even before you practice singing them. Maintain a pure vowel sound throughout the duration of the musical note value.

Author Dorothy Uris has words of advice to singers regarding diction: "reject... false notions about English consonants; word-by-word delivery that loses listeners and energy; breaking the legato of singing by careless articulation; unmotivated stops and badly placed quick breaths; an automatic response to punctuation; weakening the (musical) line by cutting off vowels too soon in advance of consonants; and the bending, crooning, scooping, sliding transitions between pitch."[4]

Problems can arise from too much tension in the mouth or jaw. Author William Shakespeare says, "rigidity of the floor of the mouth can but bring about a fixed state of the jaw. Whenever there is rigidity (of these areas), the vocal cords can only be described as displaced."[5] The tongue rises up causing tension in the mouth, or the jaw is too tight from the mouth dropping more open than is needed. This causes tension and pinches the tones. Tongue tension can cause the singer to make the pitch go sharp. Instead of dropping the chin, feel as though you are dropping the back of the tongue. Remember to keep the mouth relaxed; the tongue should lie flat. Shakespeare says, "on starting a note the singer should be as if a round object could roll down the throat unimpeded."[6]

If the voice does not have adequate breath support from the pelvis, then the mouth will try to take on the workload. It will want to become as tense as your abdomen muscles should be. As the mouth and jaw area become increasingly tense, the singing becomes increasingly difficult. It causes the unpleasant tremolo that is repulsive to listeners. The singer needs to sing a straight and steady tone.

If you recognize this tension-- if you can feel it in the mouth and jaw-- stop singing for a moment and review the steps for proper breathing. Mentally turn your attention to breathing. Start by taking deep breaths, sighing, and relaxing all over your body. After you feel relaxed then try again. Stand erect and check for correct posture. Breathe deeply and take in the air to sing, and start singing by fusing the voice with the breath. Mentally keep your attention on your energized breath deep in the pelvis.

Russell Hammar recognizes several areas of visible faults that have not been mentioned but can be addressed. They include: a bobbling larynx that can be caused by unequal tension among the muscles in the laryngeal area or faulty control of breath; the lowered larynx caused by too much opening in the oral pharynx creating a "woofy" (dark) tone; the trembling jaw caused by unequal tension between the vocal musculature and the jaw; the tucking-in of the chin is an overcompensation for lifting your chin, and can be corrected by checking your posture in front of a mirror; opening the front of your mouth too wide closes the throat; chest and shoulders that are raised too high and are rigid can be corrected by pelvic rotation and placing the body weight forward on the balls of the feet; gasping or noisy breath inhalation can be cured by opening the throat with the slight yawn.

Poor intonation, incorrect pitch, is often caused by poor breath control and poor pronunciation and focus. A flat pitch is

Back to the beginning note... mentally think it before you sing it. Mentally think through all of the tones before you sing them.

Don't back off of the breath. I can't repeat that often enough. Train the abdominal muscles to go the needed distance.

121

caused by loose breath. A sharp pitch is caused by muscle tension in the jaw and tongue. Review the chapters on breath, legato, focus of tones, and diction to learn to make corrections.

Tones which are too nasal in character, or too reedy in character, are caused by the soft palate not being raised high enough, or if there is a constriction in the oral pharynx. Make a correction by consciously lifting the soft palate higher and keeping a forward focus of tones.

Once you are singing before a listening audience, you may experience stage fright. Singers need to learn how to live with and use fear to their betterment; They need to use tension to their advantage. Turn the emotion of fear, which also brings mental alertness, into intensity of focus which brings concentration. Do this in a couple of ways: be prepared with your music; and take some action steps that bring relaxation. Breathe very deeply four or five times before you begin your performance singing. Some singers learn to drop the muscles in the neck and the abdomen to ensure that they do not seize the high tones; turning the head from one side to the other. Mentally concentrate on "what you are doing" instead of "how you are doing."

Reynaldo Hahn said, "The singer should generally refrain from excessive nuance, expression, mimicry, and modes of diction."[7]

As we are imperfect human beings, our singing experiences can vary from day to day. Difficulty in singing can be noted when you are physically tired or physically ill. At those times your body wants to breath shallowly. It does not want to breathe deeply. It is time to let your body rest. If that is not possible because of singing commitments, review the instructions over proper breathing, and try by mental concentration to breath deeply and gain cooperation from the muscles of your body.

Trust the breath.

To be a good singer you need good health. It is like being an athlete. Learn by doing. Practice everything from the beginning in a thorough and practical manner.

Kirsten Flagstad (1895-1962) Norwegian Soprano

Chapter 12
The Physiology of Singing and Vocal Ranges

The respiratory tract is a system for pulmonary ventilation. The larynx, a part of that system, provides a valve closing off the lungs and lower airways, and allowing partial closure for sound production with airflow. The thoracic rib cage with its attached muscles serving as a pump to move air in and out of the lungs.

In the upper airways, the nasal passages allow for the intake of air through the nostrils moving the air nearly halfway through the head to the pharynx. The air spaces in the bones of the face, the paranasal sinuses, serve a number of physiological purposes, but one of these purposes is the provision of resonators of the voice. Breathing through the mouth is the principle airway employed during speech or song. Beyond the pharynx lies the larynx. The vocal folds that create sound production. Between the vocal folds the airway is ordinarily triangular in shape and undergoes some widening and narrowing during breathing.

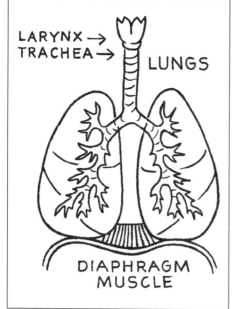

The human breathing mechanism, the breathing pump of the lungs, includes the elastic tissue of the lungs, the chest wall, the abdominal wall, and the diaphragmatic muscle, which controls the relative shape and size of the abdominal and thoracic cavaties. A number of muscles are involved in the various breathing maneuvers in which we indulge. The diaphragm is a dome shaped muscle lying between the chest and the abdomen. Its contraction flattens this dome shape and thus enlarges the thoracic cavity from below. Its action can be influenced by the various muscles of the abdominal wall which are capable of compressing the abdominal contents. Abdominal muscle contraction can push the diaphragm upward, or it can control the relative size of the thoracic cavity and shape of the abdominal contents. Between the ribs lie two sets of muscles, the internal and external intercostals. The contraction of one set, the external intercostals, elevates the ribs and increases the thoracic volume. The other set, the internal intercostals, depresses the ribs and decreases the thoracic volume.

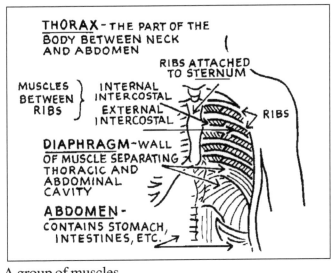

The larynx is composed of a group of cartilages held together by ligaments and muscles and suspended in the neck by muscles leading from it to the sternum and clavicle below, and the hyoid and jaw above. A group of muscles, called the constrictors, hold the larynx against the vertebrae thus closing the opening into the esophagus. Their relaxation is an essential part in swallowing. A third group of muscles closes the larynx as a valve. One muscle pair alone opens the vocal folds. The keystone of the larynx is the cricoid cartilage which forms a complete strong ring. It articulates with the thyroid and arytenoid cartilages. The ability of the laryngeal cartilages to move on one another is essential to the role of the larynx both as a valve and as an organ of phonation. The numerous muscles acting within and on the larynx work in delicate balance to achieve a lesser degree of closure of the vocal folds during phonation.

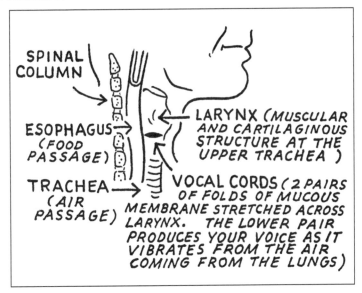

Phonation, that is sound, is caused when the column of air from the lungs passes between the closed vocal cords. The air pushes the elastic cords open, allowing a small puff of air to escape. The cords close again immediately, and the process is continued. Each time pressure builds up before the air gains enough force to push through the cords. After the air is through, there is a sudden drop in pressure. These high and low pressure areas cause waves of tension and release, which the ear drum receives and translates as sound. In essence, the emission of the air through a narrowly open glottis causes a suction that draws the cords together; more emission displaces the glottal closure and the cycle is repeated.[1]

Voice Ranges

Voices are classified by range, sex, and according to quality. Classification is made chiefly according to where the quality notes are located in the voice, and where the depth and ease of sound are located in the range. As vocal training progresses and the singer develops and matures, range usually extends and the area of true quality emerges.[2]

A. Soprano

1. coloratura- high voices; music performed is colored by ornamentation, runs, and rapid passages that require great agility. An elaborate and highly ornamented part for soprano.

2. lyric- concentrated on beauty of sound rather than range or power. The literature demands a light vocal quality and a melodious, flowing style. Music such as art songs, light operas, musical comedies, and sometimes arias in grand operas.

3. dramatic- powerful voices and pronounced histrionic ability with intense emotions; heavy orchestral accompaniment.

4. mezzo-soprano- singers lack the brilliance of higher

soprano and the richness of alto. A lower range than the lyric or coloratura soprano, but the lower range offers more fullness and intensity of tone, and often, depth of character to the voice.

B. Contralto or alto- rich, resonant, dark and throaty female voices.

C. Tenor

1. counter-tenor- a high male voice of roughly the same range as the female contralto.

2. robusto- tremendous power in the upper register often featured in Italian Opera.

3. lyric- concentrated on beauty of sound rather than range or power; the counterpart of the lyric soprano.

4. dramatic or heroic tenor- have tremendous power but associated with the German Opera. These tenors often begin their careers as high baritones, and through training and practice add to their natural range the high tones necessary to sing tenor roles.

D. Baritone

A male voice intermediate between bass and tenor. A voice that does not have extremes of range. Known for solid production and skillful interpretation.

E. Bass

A low ranged male voice. Subdivisions in this voice are predicated more upon the role or selection being sung rather than upon the characteristics of the voice.

1. basso profundo- a bass singer especially proud of the low notes.

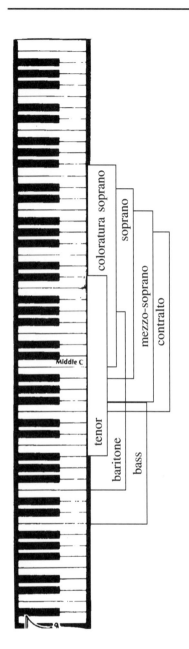

2. bass-baritone - a singer whose range encompasses that of a bass and baritone combined, or who lacks the extreme range of either one.

3. basso cantante- a bass singer specializing in a lyric style.

4. basso buffo - a bass singer associated with the comic roles of opera.

Singers in operatic roles must perform the parts as they are written to be integrated with the dramatic content and musical expression of the orchestra and the other singers. Singers are selected for operatic roles on the basis of having a voice that fits the part. They concentrate their efforts on a limited number of roles for which their voices are best suited.

The approximate functional ranges of the various voices as indicated on the piano keyboard are:

Upper case letters are below the octave below Middle C;

Lower case letters are above Middle C and the first octave below Middle C;

Middle C is marked as c'; the octave below that is c. The markings that follow the alphabet letters indicate the octave that the musical note is found moving either direction on the piano keyboard. Lower case letters move up in pitch on the piano keyboard, and upper case letters move down in pitch on the piano keyboard.

Coloratura or high soprano- c' to f'''

Soprano- b' to d'''

Mezzo-Soprano- g to b'''

Contralto- f to g''

Tenor- b to c''

Baritone- F to g'

Bass- C to f'

There are two extremes in vocal ranges: Stroh bass, notes that are below the ledger line of the bass clef; and whistle tones of soprano at b flat 3 or above. This soprano range is also called flageolet or bell register.

Vocal timbre or coloration is synonymous with tone quality. In German it is called tone color. These terms may be defined as the quality or tone identity of musical sound, as determined by the number and the character of its overtones. The number and character of these overtones are determined by the size, shape, and texture of their corresponding resonators, plus the degree of intensity of the tone. The quality is inherent in the individual's physical make-up.[3]

Chapter 13
Further Study in Pronunciation
Suggested Vocal Exercises and Solo Music

In singing in various languages you should acquire a European raised speech. Whenever possible study languages with those individuals who are well spoken in each language. The knowledge and use of the Italian language is most desireable. For singers it is best suited to consistently good tone production. "Italian may be said to be a language consisting mainly of sustained vowels and of consonants from which all awkward combinations have been eliminated. By sustaining the vowels and simplifying the consonants a language has been formed which is in itself an education in the freedom of action of both the tongue and the throat. This freedom of utterance becomes an inestimable value in the production of pure tone," says author Shakespeare.[1]

When singing in the German language, use the pronunciation known as "Schönbruner German."

Let us consider a closer examination of pronunciation of the vowels and consonants as they are used in the formation of the words in singing in the English language. The English language in conversation does not lend itself to the prolongation required in finding the exact sounds for singing, as singing is a measured and sustained form of speech.

The different sounds derived from the five vowels are described as long and short, or open and closed. To simplify the description of the English vowel sounds, which are thirteen in number, they have been written here exactly as they sound phonetically:[2]

ah is vowel sound I., as in the words *are, bar, guard*.

aᵗ is vowel sound II., as in the words *as, bat, cab, damp, fan, gas*. The vowel sound in the word *at* could not be described without the addition of some terminal consonant, a small *t* is printed after it whenever this particular vowel sound is in question, but the *t* is not intended to be pronounced.

a, vowel sound III., is a dipthong—that is to say, it is composed of two sounds which succeed each other rapidly, as in the words *bay, cane, dame, eight, reign, fail*. To describe separately the two sounds of this dipthong in writing is difficult, because in English the first sound does not occur alone, but if separately prolonged, would result in French as the open *e*, as in *meme, reve*; it also occurs in certain Italian words, and is represented in German by the modified *a*, as in *Mädchen*. The second sound can be described as that which is heard in the word it, a sound which without the *t* will afterwards be known as vowel sound V. The above word *bay* is pronounced *ba-i*ᵗ. Remember that the first sound of this dipthong is that which is accented.

air is the variety of the above dipthong, which is heard when the second sound consists of **u**ᵗ . (This **u**ᵗ will be known later as vowel sound XIII.; the *t* is not pronounced.) It occurs in *air, care, bear, rare, fair*, and commences with the first sound of **a**, but the last sound is that of **u**ᵗ . Let the first sound receive the accent.

eᵗ is vowel sound IV., and must be pronounced without the *t*. It is heard in the words *any, every, best, debt, fell, hemp*. It is almost identical with the closed *e* of the French and Italian languages.

iᵗ is vowel sound V. (The *t* is not to be pronounced.) It is heard in *it, bid, din, fill, is, kiss*, and in the second syllable of *any, money, hymn*, and at the end of the dipthong **a**, vowel sound III. above.

ee is vowel sound VI., as in *bead, feel, ease, key, fiend, scheme*.

oo is vowel sound VII., as in *hoot, coo, doom, food, who, true, shoe*.

^h**oo**^d is vowel sound VIII., and is pronounced with the lips not quite so much pursed as for vowel sound VII. It is described in the sound heard in the word *hood*, because no shorter formula can be found. Neither *h* nor *d* should be pronounced, and for the reason both are written small. This vowel sound occurs in the words *full, should*. The distinction between ^h**oo**^d and **oo** may be observed in such phrases as *"a pool full," "they could coo," "he would woo," "he should shoe."*

o is vowel sound IX., and is a dipthong as regards which English-speaking nations find great difficulty is separating the first sound from the second. In English we always end this dipthong with the vowel sound ^h**oo**^d, No. VIII. We must practice until we can prolong *o* without the final ^h**oo**^d. The vowel sound **o** occurs in *owe, bowl, coal, roll, hole, woe, though*. The accent must always be on the first sound of the dipthong.

aw is vowel sound X., as in *all, bawl, balk, jaw, corn, lawn*. English singers often have trouble with this vowel, and are prone to hold the throat rigidly, whereas it should be only slightly and unconsciously contracted for its pronunciation.

o^t is vowel sound XI. The *t* is written small and is not intended to be sounded. This vowel occurs in *cot, dog, God, hop, gloss*.

er is vowel sound XII. The *r* is not to be trilled, but is merely a sign like the *t*, by which to recognize the vowel sound. It occurs in *burr, mirth, earl, fur, hurl, jerk*.

u^t is vowel sound XIII. The *t* is not to be sounded. It occurs in *but, cup, dull, fun, love, rough*.

The remaining dipthongs are as follows:

I-dipthong is a dipthong involving a rapid change of tongue position from **ah** (vowel No. I.) to **i**^{t} (vowel No. V.) It is heard in the words *my, thy, tie, sky, buy*. In the first word, for instance, it may be written out as **mah-i**^{t}. The accent must fall on the first sound.

ou. This dipthong, which is heard in *bough, cow, fowl, now, thou*. The sound consists of **u**^{t} (vowel No. XIII.) and by ^{h}**oo**^{d} (vowel No. VIII.) The accent falls on the first sound.

oi is a dipthong consisting of **aw** (vowel No. X.) followed by **i**^{t} (vowel No. V.), the accent resting on the first sound. It occurs in *oil* and *boy*.

u and **y**. The vowel sound **i**^{t} can combine in English with any of the other vowel sounds to form a dipthong, in which the accent is invariably on the second sound. When the first sound, **i**^{t}, commences a syllable, it is generally written *y*— e.g., *yarn, yea, ye, yes, you, yacht, yore, yoke*. The most common of these dipthongs is the combination of **i**^{t} and **oo** (vowel No. VII.), which is usually represented in English by *u*, though there are other ways of writing it— e.g., *use, cure, tune, few, beauty*. Remember that *u* may also represent **oo** (vowel No. VII.), as in *true*, or ^{h}**oo**^{d} (vowel No. VIII.) as in *bull*; and *y* may represent **i**^{t} alone, as in *any*, or i-dipthong, as in *rhyme*.

w. Similarly the vowel sound VIII., ^{h}**oo**^{d}, may combine with any of the other vowel sounds to form a dipthong, having an accent on the second syllable. It is represented by *w* in English, and further allows for the introduction of an aspirate between the two sounds— e.g., *wan, wed, which*.

On the selection of vowel sounds in certain words when sustained in singing:

the. The definite article, when it proceeds the vowel sounds *a, e, i*, and *o*, should be pronounced with a long *e* such as in the word thee, in words such as th*ee* apple, th*ee* egg, th*ee* inn; but when it precedes a *u*, or it precedes a consonant, it is pronounced th*u*ᵗ (No. XIII. above), in words such as th*u*ᵗ use, th*u*ᵗ bee, th*u*ᵗ heart.

a. The indefinite article always takes the sound of **u**ᵗ (vowel No. XIII.) in English. In words like **u**ᵗ bee, **u**ᵗ jest, **u**ᵗ few.

my. The possessive pronoun *my* should be pronounced *mah-i*ᵗ, that is vowels No. I. and No. V. whenever it has to be sustained on a long note. However, when it has a short note, and the emphasis is on the following word, it may be pronounced *mi*ᵗ, vowel No. V., as in *mi*ᵗ child, *mi*ᵗ wife.

r. Although the *r* is trilled or rolled when it precedes a vowel, yet it is not often rolled otherwise, but takes the sound of **u**ᵗ (vowel No. XIII.). The words *air, butter, cellar, ever, flower, member, war*, should be pronounced *a-u*ᵗ (not *ai-er* nor *airr*), *buttu*ᵗ, *cellu*ᵗ,... etc. In other words such as *car, darn, earl,* and *girl*, the *r* of course is not rolled. (see vowel sounds No.I and No. VII.).

The Buzzes are as follows:

In English they are soft *th, v, z*, and the French *j*, occurring in English in only a few words such as the word *treasure*. The role that they play in pronunciation is remarkable. If they are not pronounced sufficiently, the result is that we cannot tell what the singer or actor is saying. If the rigid singer fails to soften his musical line, he produces harsh and sibilant tones (hissing sounds).

Buzz No. I. There are two ways of pronouncing *th*. One is the soft *th*, a buzzing sound which can only be executed when the tongue is perfectly free, as in the words *thou, thy, this, with, father*. The second way of pronouncing *th* is the hard *th*, as in the words *thatch, thimble, thicket, thing*. Examples of the difference between the soft *th* and the hard *th* may be seen in such phrases as "*Thou* hast a *thousand*," or "*Thy thigh* is broken," or "*This* is a *thistle*."

Buzz No. II. is *v*, as in *vane, vanish, sever, wave*. Only a good singer can sustain this buzz; the bad singer is forced to either omit it or to substitute the hissing consonant *f*.

Buzz No. III. is *z*, as in *zeal, easy, haze, bays, was*. This sound is extremely important because under it are included nearly all plural substantives in the English language, and also for the most part the third person singular of verbs.

Buzz No. IV. is only heard in the middle of English words, but occurs very often in French in the form of *j* and *g*, as in the words *j'ai* and *juge*. In English it is written with with an *s* or a *z*. It is heard in such words as *measure, pleasure, azure, treasure*.

These four buzzes when spoken correctly by the singer reduces all rigidity of voice production and brings forth a sense of velvety smoothness and harmony which are heard frequently in poetry.

Hints on other consonants:

Practice the consonants *l, d, t, n, r*, hard *g*, and *k*, and the buzz *th*, until they can be clearly pronounced without movement of the jaw. Sing with the lips free so that *m* is not a hard, tight sound.

Acquire a mastery over the trilling or rolling of the *r*. It must be executed by a rapid vibration of the tip of the tongue against the front upper teeth. Practice pronouncing words like *crush* or *press* or *trill* until the singer develops a habit of looseness of the tip of the tongue.

The sound of *s* must not be agressively heard, but should be a soft sound that moves in the direction of the teeth as in whistling. Recall that rigidity of the lips prevents the free pronunciation of the hisses: *s, f, ch, sh*, and the hard *th*.

Pronounce clearly the final *n, ng*, and *l* in such words as *thing*.

Suggested Vocal Exercises

In addition to the exercises suggested in the beginning chapters of instructions, here are some additional exercises that can be used for vocal warm-ups.

With this exercise use the following consonants and vowels as syllables--

Lo-o-Lah-ah-Lee-e-e-e-e

Start this exercise in the key of C Major. The beginning note will be middle C for women, an octave below that for men. Do the exercise up and down the major diatonic scale from that starting point.

Substitute consonants in the above exercise. Substitute an "M" for the "L". So the syllables would sound--

Mo-o-Mah-ah-Mee-e-e-e-e.

On another occasion substitute an "N" for the "L" in the syllables.

Another exercise with nine tones in the major diatonic scale. With this exercise use the following consonants and vowels as syllables--

Lo-o-o-o-Lah-ah-ah-ah-lee-e-e-e-e-e-e-e.

You can use the C Major scale as a starting tone. Once again take the vocal exercise up and down the major diatonic scale.

This vocal exercise can also use the consonants of "N" and "M" substituted for the "L." The choice of those consonants is to help the singer in placing the tones, that is focusing the tones, high in the facial mask.

Grand Arpeggio

a- o- a- o- a- o- a- o-a- o-a- o- a-   ah----

a- o- a- o- a- o- a- o-a- o-a- o- a-   ah----

a- o- a- o- a- o- a- o-a- o-a- o- a-   ah----

a- o- a- o- a- o- a- o-a- o-a- o- a-   ah----

a- o- a- o- a- o- a- o-a- o-a- o- a-   ah----

a- o- a- o- a- o- a- o-a- o-a- o- a-   ah----

Exercise with Key Change

Exercise with Rapid Passages

Suggested Printed Music for Beginning Solo Voices

There are many fine music publishers. This listing is only intended as an introduction and a guide for beginning singers. Visit a sheet music store for a wide range of choices.

Vaccai—Practical Method of Italian Singing
Schirmer's Library of Musical Classics
Soprano or high soprano, tenor, alto or baritone

The First Book of Soprano Solos
G.Schirmer Publisher
Available in other voice ranges: Mezzo-Soprano/Alto; Tenor; Baritone/Bass

The Second Book of Soprano Solos
G. Schirmer Publisher
Available in other voice ranges

Twenty-Four Italian Songs and Arias
Composers of the 17th and 18th century with English and Italian texts
Schirmer's Library of Musical Classics,
In medium high or medium low voice ranges

Twenty-Six Italian Songs and Arias
Containing some of the world's most famous Italian songs and arias
Schirmer's Library of Musical Classics,
In medium high or medium low voice ranges

The Young Singer
Collection of varied and artistic selection of songs from many nationalities and eras.
Carl Fischer Publisher
Soprano, Contralto, Tenor, and Baritone/Bass

Folk Songs for Solo Singers
Arranged by Jay Althouse
    Alfred Publication
    In medium high or medium low voice ranges

Songs of John Jacob Niles
America's folk songs
    G. Schirmer Publisher,
    In medium and low voice ranges

NOTES

Chapter 5
(1) William Shakespeare, <u>The Art of Singing</u> (Oliver Ditson Company, 1921), p.9

Chapter 6
(1) William Shakespeare, <u>The Art of Singing</u> (Oliver Ditson Company, 1921), p.14
(2) William Shakespeare, <u>The Art of Singing</u> (Oliver Ditson Company, 1921), p.19, p.24

Chapter 7
(1) Meribeth Bunch, <u>Dynamics of the Singing Voice</u> (Publisher Springer-Verlag/Wien, 1982), p.93

Chapter 8
(1) William Shakespeare, <u>The Art of Singing</u> (Oliver Ditson Company, 1921), p. 43
(2) Dorothy Uris, <u>To Sing In English- A Guide to Improved Diction</u> (New York, Boosey and Hawkes, 1971), p. 14
(3) Dorothy Uris, <u>To Sing In English- A Guide to Improved Diction</u> (New York, Boosey and Hawkes, 1971), p. 15
(4) Dorothy Uris, <u>To Sing In English- A Guide to Improved Diction</u> (New York, Boosey and Hawkes, 1971), p. 68
(5) Russell A. Hammar, <u>Singing - An Extension of Speech</u>, (Scarecrow Press, 1978), p. 62
(6) Russell A. Hammar, <u>Singing - An Extension of Speech</u>, (Scarecrow Press, 1978), p. 85
(7) Russell A. Hammar, <u>Singing - An Extension of Speech</u>, (Scarecrow Press, 1978), p. 16
(8) Russell A. Hammar, <u>Singing - An Extension of Speech</u>, (Scarecrow Press, 1978), pages 122 and 123
(9) Russell A. Hammar, <u>Singing - An Extension of Speech</u>, (Scarecrow Press, 1978), p. 11
(10) William Shakespeare, <u>The Art of Singing</u> (Oliver Ditson Company, 1921), p. 43

Chapter 9
(1) William Shakespeare, <u>The Art of Singing</u>, (Oliver Ditson Company, 1921), p. 27
(2) Reynaldo Hahn, <u>On Singers and Singing</u>, (Portland, Oregon, Amadeus Press, 1990), p. 94
(3) Russell A. Hammar, <u>Singing - An Extension of Speech</u>, (Scarecrow Press, 1978), p. 66 and p. 169
(4) Reynaldo Hahn, <u>On Singers and Singing</u>, (Portland, Oregon, Amadeus Press, 1990), p. 26
(5) William Shakespeare, <u>The Art of Singing</u>, (Oliver Ditson Company, 1921), p. 39
(6) Meribeth Bunch, <u>Dynamics of the Singing Voice</u>, (Springer-Verlag/Wien, 1982), p. 71
(7) Meribeth Bunch, <u>Dynamics of the Singing Voice</u>, (Springer-Verlag/Wien, 1982) p. 72

Chapter 10
(1) William Shakespeare, <u>The Art of Singing</u>, (Oliver Ditson Company, 1921), p. 24
(2) William Shakespeare, <u>The Art of Singing</u>, (Oliver Ditson Company, 1921), p. 27, 28
(3) William Shakespeare, <u>The Art of Singing</u>, (Oliver Ditson Company, 1921), p. 29
(4) William Shakespeare, <u>The Art of Singing</u>, (Oliver Ditson Company, 1921), p. 40
(5) Reynaldo Hahn, <u>On Singers and Singing</u>, (Portland, Oregon, Amadeus Press, 1990), p. 126

Chapter 11
(1) Meribeth Bunch, <u>Dynamics of the Singing Voice</u>, (Springer-Verlag/Wien, 1982), p. 68
(2) Russell A. Hammar, <u>Singing- An Extension of Speech</u>, (Scarecrow Press, 1978), p. 84
(3) Reynaldo Hahn, <u>On Singers and Singing</u>, (Portland, Oregon, Amadeus Press, 1990), p. 208
(4) Dorothy Uris, <u>To Sing In English- A Guide To Improved Diction</u>, (New York, Boosey and Hawkes, 1971), p. 68
(5) William Shakespeare, <u>The Art of Singing</u>, (Oliver Ditson Company, 1921), p. 24
(6) William Shakespeare, <u>The Art of Singing</u>, (Oliver Ditson Company, 1921), p. 23
(7) Reynaldo Hahn, <u>On Singers and Singing</u>, (Portland, Oregon, Amadeus Press, 1990), p. 153

Chapter 12
(1) William D. Leyerle, <u>Vocal Development Through Organic Imagery</u>, (State University of New York, 1986), p. 21
(2) Meribeth Bunch, <u>Dynamics of the Singing Voice</u>, (Springer-Verlag/Wien, 1982), p. 67
(3) William D. Leyerle, <u>Vocal Development Through Organic Imagery</u>, (State University of New York, 1986), p. 80

Chapter 13
(1) William Shakespeare, <u>The Art of Singing</u> (Oliver Ditson Company, 1921), p. 43
(2) William Shakespeare, <u>The Art of Singing</u> (Oliver Ditson Company, 1921), p. 167

BIBLIOGRAPHY

Apel, Willi. <u>Harvard Dictionary of Music</u> (The Belknap Press of Harvard University Press, Cambridge, Massachusetts, 1972).

Brown, William Earl. <u>Vocal Wisdom</u> (Arno Press, Inc., New York, NY, 1957).

Bunch, Meribeth. <u>Dynamics of the Singing Voice</u> (Springer-Verlag/Wien, 1982).

Covington, Richard. "The Aria Never Ends in the Opera That's Casa Verdi," *Smithsonian*, Vol. 26, Dec. 1995.

Douglas, Nigel. <u>Legendary Voices</u> (CD) (Nimbus Records Limited, Charlottesville, VA, 1993).

Edwards, Betty. <u>Drawing on the Right Side of the Brain: A Course in Enhancing Creativity and Artistic Confidence</u> (J.P. Tarcher, Inc., Los Angeles, CA, 1979).

Fife, Austin E. <u>Heaven on Horseback: Revivalist Songs and Verse in the Cowboy Idiom</u> (Utah State University Pres, UT, 1989).

Fink, Kathy and Tod Whittemore. <u>Learn to Yodel</u> (audiotape), Homespun Tapes, Woodstock, NY, 1985.

Flanagan, Bill. <u>Written in My Soul</u> (Oxford University Press, 1987).

Friedman, Judith Kate. "Creativity at Any Age," *Acoustic Guitar Magazine*, Vol. 7 Issue 48, Dec. 1996.

<u>Great Opera Stars in Historic Photographs</u>. Edited by James Camner, (Dover Publications, New York, NY, 1978).

Hahn, Reynaldo. <u>On Singers and Singing</u> (Amadeus Press, Portland, OR, 1990).

Handy, W. C. <u>Father of the Blues</u> (McMillan Company, NY, 1941).

Hansen, George. "Blue Highways: Meet Honeyboy Edwards, a Living Link to the Original Delta Blues," *Acoustic Guitar Magazine*, Vol. 7, Issue 48, Dec. 1996.

Hammar, Russell A. <u>Singing- An Extension of Speech</u> (Scarecrow Press, 1978).

Hulbert, Henry Harper. <u>Breathing for Voice Production</u> (Novello, 1903).

Judy, Stephanie. <u>Making Music for the Joy of It</u> (Jeremy P. Tarcher/Putnam Book, New York, NY, 1990).

Lee, Katie. <u>Ten Thousand Goddamned Cattle</u> (Northland Press, Flagstaff, AZ, 1976).

Leyerle, William D. <u>Vocal Development Through Organic Imagery</u> (State University of New York, NY, 1986).

Ohrlin, Glenn. <u>The Hellbound Train, a Cowboy Songbook</u> (University of Illinois Press, Urbana, Chicago, London, 1973).

Proctor, Donald, MD. <u>Breathing, Speech, and Song</u> (Springer-Verlag/Wien, 1980).

Ristad, Eloise. <u>A Soprano On Her Head: Right-side-up Reflections on Life and Other Performances</u> (Real People Press, Moab, UT, 1982).

Rainbolt, Jo. <u>The Last Cowboy</u> (American & World Geographic Publishing, Helena, MT, 1992).

Seeger, Tony. "When We Stop Singing, We Will Really be Finished," *Smithsonian Magazine*, Vol. 27, May 1996.

Shakespeare, William. <u>The Art of Singing</u> (Oliver Ditson Company, 1921).

Small, Mark L. "Face to Face with Pat Metheny," *Acoustic Guitar Magazine*, Vol.7 Issue 52, April 1997.

Tinsley, Bob. For A Cowboy Has to Sing: A Collection of 60 Romantic and Cowboy Western Songs (University of Central Florida Press, Orlando, FL, 1991).

Turner, Jessica Baron. "Good Vibrations," *Acoustic Guitar Magazine*, Vol. 7 Issue 48, Dec. 1996.

Ulrich, Homer. Famous Women Singers (Dodd, Mead & Co. New York, 1953).

Uris, Dorothy. To Sing in English- A Guide to Improved Diction (New York, Boosey and Hawkes, 1971).

White, John I. Git Along Little Dogies, Songs and Songmakers of the American West. (University of Illinois Press, 1975).

GLOSSARY

a cappella—for unaccompanied voices. Designation for choral music without instrumental accompaniment. Originally the name referred to unaccompanied church music.

accelerando—gradually becoming faster.

accent—in musical notation, a sign above a note indicating that the note should be sung or played with a strong stress or accent applied at the beginning of the note.

acciaccatura—a vocal embellishment, an ornamental note; the singing of a neighboring tone, usually the lower second interval, to a normally written note of the melody; the neighboring tone is sung quickly and released immediately. Commonly referred to as a grace note.

accidentals—the signs used in musical notation to indicate chromatic alterations from the written key signature of music as applied to a single note; or to cancel an alteration used earlier in the written music.

adagio—a leisurely slow tempo, faster than lento and slower than andante.

allegro—a cheerful, rapid, brisk tempo.

andante—a moderate, flowing, or walking tempo.

appoggiatura—a vocal embellishment, an ornamental note, usually a lower second, that is melodically connected with the main note that follows it and sung in the same breath. When sung, the appoggiatura takes half of the value of the succeeding note.

aria—a lyric song with instrumental accompaniment. An elaborate composition for solo voice most frequently recognized with opera to the end of the 19th century, and with cantatas and oratorios of the 17th and 18th centuries.

arietta—a small aria lacking the musical elaboration of the aria, rather a song or a cavatina.

arpeggio—the notes of a music chord played one after another instead of simultaneously.

art song—an independent song for solo voice and piano developed during the romantic era of music history combining a poem and melody. A song of serious artistic intent written by a trained composer.

a tempo—return to the original tempo of the music.

bel canto—the Italian vocal technique of the 18th century, with its emphasis on beauty of sound and brilliance of performance rather than dramatic expresssion or romantic emotion. It is considered a highly artistic technique and the only proper one for Italian opera and Mozart. More recently the term bel canto has been associated with a mid-17th-century development represented by L. Rossi (1597-1653) and G. Carissimi (1605-74), who cultivated a simple, melodious vocal style of songlike quality, without virtuoso coloraturas.

cadence—a melodic or harmonic formula that occurs at the end of a musical phrase, section, or composition conveying the impression of a momentary or permanent conclusion. Also, a 17th century name for the trill.

cadenza—a passage or section of music of varying length in a style of brilliant improvisation, usually near the end of a composition, giving the performer a chance to exhibit his technical mastery.

cantata—a composite vocal form of the baroque period, consisting of a number of movements which are based on a continuous narrative text that is lyrical, dramatic, or religious. The movements consist of arias, recitatives, duets and choruses.

cavatina—a short solo song in opera and oratorios that is simpler in style than the aria and without repetition of words or phrases, used in the 18th and 19th centuries.

choir—a body of church singers, as opposed to a secular chorus. The name is also used for instrumental groups of the orchestra, e.g., brass choir, string choir, woodwind choir.

choral music—vocal music for more than one singer with or without instrumental accompaniment. The music may consist of a single voice part or a number of voice parts.

chromatic scale—use of all twelve consecutive half-step notes of each octave ascending or descending.

coda—an ending added to a movement or composition.

consonance—a musical sound which is stable and which does not have the urgency to resolve. Consonant intervals are the perfect intervals and the major and minor third intervals and sixth intervals.

counterpoint—music consisting of two or more melody lines that sound simultaneously; melody against melody.

crescendo—gradually increasing in loudness.

da capo (D.C.)—from the beginning. The composition is to be repeated from the beginning.

dal segno (D.S.)—from the sign. The composition is to be repeated from the sign.

decrescendo, or diminuendo—gradually growing softer.

diatonic scale—the natural scale consisting of five whole tones (whole steps) and two semitones (half steps) of an octave in a fixed form of step, step, half-step, step, step, step, half-step, with consecutive alphabet letter names.

diphthong—a union of two vowels pronounced in one syllable.

dissonance—a musical sound which is unstable, more active, and which needs to resolve to a consonant interval.

dolce—sweet and soft.

dynamics—musical volume. Denotes the degree of loudness or softness at which the music is played or sung.

expressivo—with expression.

falsetto—an artificial method of singing used by male singers, particularly tenors, to reach notes above their ordinary range. It is an action that deliberately limits the tone-making apparatus. Such tones are rather weak when compared with the normal tones of a voice.

fermata—a hold or pause.

fine—an indication of the end of a composition after a D.C. or a D.S. sign.

forte (f)—loud in dynamics.

fortissimo (ff)—very loud in dynamics.

glottis—The opening at the upper part of the windpipe of the human body, and between the vocal cords, which by its dilation and contraction contributes to the modulation of the voice.

giusto—strict and exact.

grave—solemn, serious and slow.

gruppetto—a vocal embellishment, ornamental notes; a group of three or four notes that turn around a principal note. Starting on the principal note, moving to the note above the principal note, then return to the principal note, then move to the note below the principal note, then move back to the principal note. Performed as four equal notes taking up the whole time value of the written note. Also called the turn.

harmonics—secondary tones which form a component of every musical sound, though they are not heard distinctly.

harmony—musical space. Harmony adds depth to melody. The vertical structure or chordal structure of a musical composition.

history of music—
1) Middle Ages, Romanesque, Gothic, up to 1450;
2) Renaissance, 1450 to 1600;
3) Baroque, 1600 to 1750;
4) Rococo, 1725 to 1775;
5) Classical, 1775 to 1825;
6) Romantic, 1820 to 1900;
7) Post-Romantic, including Impressionism, 1890 to 1915;
8) Twentieth Century, 1910 to present.

improvisation—the singer or player adding his own embellishments to what was written down in printed music. The art of performing music spontaneously, without the aid of manuscript or memory.

intervals—The relationship between two pitches. The distance in pitch between two tones or notes. A measurement of the tonal space between two notes. The name of each interval indicates the number of tones of the diatonic scale.

intonation—process of singing on pitch; singing or playing in tune, particularly in ensemble performance.

keynote—The central note of the key of music; the first degree of the scale in tonal music; the tonic note.

largamente—broadly.

largo—a slow, broad, stately tempo, slower than lento.

legato— for a singer, carrying one tone into another tone without interruption of the breath. A smooth and connected manner of playing or singing with no separation between notes. To be played without any perceptible interruption between the notes.

leggero, leggiero—lightly.

lento—a slow tempo, but not as slow as largo.

libretto—the text of an opera or oratorio.

lied—an art song of the Romantic period of music history; a song in the German vernacular, belonging to the speech of the everyday idiom of the Germans.

lyric—(adj.) smoothness of melody. Lyrical music is the union of music and poetry that expresses human emotion ranging from tender sentiment to dramatic balladry.

lyrics—(noun) the words or text of a song.

maestoso—majestically.

major interval—music intervals of the major thirds and sixths (imperfect consonance); and major seconds and sevenths, and the perfect fourth when not supported by a third or perfect fifth below it (dissonant intervals).

major scale—a set of eight notes contained within an octave that follow a fixed form of step, step, half-step, step, step, step, half-step, with consecutive alphabet letter names.

melody—musical line. A succession of musical tones perceived by the mind as unity. Melody represents the horizontal element of musical texture of motion and rhythm.

messa di voce—a special vocal technique of 18th century "bel canto," consisting of a gradual crescendo and decrescendo over a sustained tone. A singer commencing a note in a very soft voice, increasing its force and intensity in the highest possible degree, and then returning without loss of quality to very soft voice again.

mezzo forte (mf)—moderately loud in dynamics.

mezzo piano (mp)—moderately soft in dynamics.

mezza voce—sung with half voice.

minor scale—harmonic minor: a set of eight notes contained within an octave that follow a fixed form of step, half-step, step, step, half-step, half-step, one and one-half step, half step, with consecutive alphabet letter names. Melodic minor scale: a set of eight notes contained within an octave that follow a fixed form of ascending pattern of step, half-step, step, step, step, step, half-step; descending pattern of step, step, half-step, step, step, half-step, step, with consecutive alphabet letter names.

moderato—a moderate tempo.

mordent—a vocal embellishment, an ornamentation, consisting of the alteration of the written note, after it is first sung, with the singing of the note immediately below it, then return to the original written note. The mordent always occupies part of the note value of the written note when performed.

morendo—dying away, growing softer and softer.

musical notation—the method used for writing down music to indicate the two main properties of musical sound: its pitch and its duration. The musical note indicates pitch by its position on a staff provided with a clef. Duration of music notes is provided by a variety of shapes, such as hollow or black heads on notes, with or without stems or flags. Other musical symbols are key signature, time signature, tempo marks, dynamic marks, and expression marks.

opera—an artistic form that combines music and theatrical representation. A drama in which music is the essential factor comprising songs with orchestral accompaniment and orchestral preludes and interludes. It is highly complex, involving many different arts-instrumental and vocal music, drama, poetry, dance, stage design, and costuming.

opus—a term used to indicate the chronological position of a composition within a composer's entire output of works.

oratorio—a musical composition with long libretto of religious or contemplative character that is performed in a concert hall or church without scenery, costumes, or action, by a chorus, solo voices, and orchestra.

passagi—a point of voice register transition; a passage from one voice register to another.

perfect intervals—music intervals of unisons, octaves, fifths and fourths.

pianissimo (pp)— very soft in dynamics.

piano (p)—soft in dynamics.

pitch—the location of a musical sound in the tonal scale; the pitch is determined by the rate of vibration, the number of vibrations per second of the sound.

piu—(It.) more

poco—(It.) little

portamento—occurs when a singer moves from one note to another. The singer slides the voice from one note to the other, touching on, but not stopping on, all the intermediate notes rather than moving the voice cleanly from one note to another. In an effective portamento, the singer must so blend the different registers and so bind the notes that they seem to flow into one even tone.

Portamento means carrying up or down of the vowel sound to another note where a change of word or syllable occurs.

presto—a very fast tempo.

rallentando—gradually growing slower.

recitative—a vocal style usually employed with narrative prose texts, particularly in operas, also oratorios, where it serves to carry the action from one aria to another. A vocal style designed to imitate and emphasize the natural inflections of speech. In opera a speechlike reiteration of the same note, slight inflections, irregular rhythms, and purely syllabic treatment of the text.

registers—the different portions of the vocal range which are distinguished according to their place of production and sound quality: low register (chest); middle register; high register (head).

resonation—reinforcement of vibration of sound. Resonators are bodies that react with sounds of any frequency or pitch. With the human voice the resonators are in the head and chest.

rhythm—musical time. The controlled movement of music in time. The duration of the tones, the frequency, and the regularity or irregularity with which the tones are sounded in a musical passage. In a primary sense, rhythm is the whole feeling of movement in music.

ritardando—gradually growing slower, holding back.

ritenuto—immediately growing slower.

rubato—rhythmic freedom of a beat or measure in which time values are taken from one and given to another for expressive purposes.

scale passages, rapid passages—sections of music that contain a brilliant display of virtuosity usually sung quickly.

scherzando—playfully.

secular music—music not devoted to sacred or religious use; temporal or worldy music.

sforzando—sudden stress; accent on a single note or chord. (sf is the symbol)

solfeggio—vocal exercises sung to a vowel, or to the syllables of solmization (do, re, mi, fa, so, la, ti, do) without text.

solo—a piece executed by one performer, either alone, or with accompaniment by an instrument.

song—a short lyric composition for solo voice based on a poetic text. The vocal melody has instrumental accompaniment that gives it harmonic background and support.

sostenuto—sustained, usually in a fairly slow tempo.

staccato—a manner of performance placed by a dot over a musical note, indicating that the note should be shortened in duration and detached from the next note. The reduction in the duration of the written musical note would be with a rest of one-half duration or more of its value.

strident tone—a vocal tone that is shrill or harsh.

subito (It.)—suddenly.

tempo—musical pace. The rate of speed of the music. The speed of a composition ranging from very slow to very fast as indicated by tempo marks.

tenuto—hold, to sustain its full value.

tessitura—the general range of pitch within which most of the tones of a composition fall, or which can be encompassed by a singer's voice. It differs from vocal range in that it does not take into account a few isolated notes of extraordinarily high or low pitch.

timbre—vocal timbre or coloration--the tone quality, or tone color, or tone identity, of musical sound as determined by the number and character of its overtones (harmonics). The number and character of the harmonics are determined by the size, shape, and texture of their corresponding resonators, and the degree of intensity of the tone.

tone—a sound of definite pitch and duration. The quality of the sound production in a voice. Also, can be used to mean a "whole tone" the interval of a major second of a musical scale.

tone color—the quality of a tone as produced on a specific instrument, as distinct from the different quality of the same tone if played on some other instrument; tone color is determined by the harmonics, or the greater or lesser prominence of one or another harmonic.

transpose—to rewrite a piece of music in a different key.

tremolo—in voice it is the excessive vibrato that leads to deviation of pitch. Vibrato of more than eight pulsations per second; a fast and frantic vibrato. It results from the lack of breath control and faulty control of the singing muscles causing too much presure on the vocal folds.

trill—a vocal embellishment, a vocal ornament, consisting of the rapid alteration of a given note with the diatonic scale second interval above it. An embellishment consisting of the principal note which necessarily belongs to the harmony of the composition, sung in rapid alternation with the note of the scale next above it.

vibrato—in vocal music, a tone which fluctuates smoothly andproportionally in the three areas of pitch, intensity, and timbre, that is usually about six to seven times per second at one-quarter-step above and one-quarter-step below the center of the pitch. A tremelo vibrates too fast. A wobble vibrates too slowly and irregularly.

vivace—a quick, lively tempo.

vocalises—a long melody sung on a vowel without text; a singer can concentrate on using pure tone in the sense of the instrumentalist, unimpeded by words, for expressive purposes. The added hazard of a text is eliminated until the sensation of making a pure tone has been firmly established.

voce (It.)—voice.

voice ranges—human voices are usually divided into six ranges: three female voices of soprano, mezzo-soprano, and contralto, and three male voices of tenor, baritone, and bass.

wobble—an excessively slow vibrato less than five pulsations per second, an undesireable vocal characteristic. It is caused by muscle fatigue, emotional tension or excessive contraction of muscles of the larynx.

INDEX

A

abdomen 90-91, 98, 100, 108, 110, 112, 118-119, 121-122
Alexie, Sherman 7
altered state 6, 56
amateur 7
Anderson, Marian 44
Argo, Arthur 6
articulation 102, 120
authority 27, 52, 70
Autry, Gene 62
awareness 5, 63, 73, 78
Axton, Hoyt 64

B

Baez, Joan 29, 38, 48, 62
Baratella, Fedora 48
Beighle, Richard 33
Bel Canto 115
belly 42, 58, 77, 78
birth of the blues 52
Bitterroot Valley 62
Bjorling, Jussi 46
blacks 10, 20, 38, 49
Blake, William 3
Bland, James 49
Bloxham, Earsel 62
blues 7, 9, 15, 42, 50, 51, 52, 53, 56, 61, 63
Bly, Robert 5
breath energy 93, 108, 113, 114
breathing 90, 91, 97, 108, 118, 121, 122, 124
Broschi, Carlo 25
Brown, William Earl 21
Butler, Virginia 9, 50

E

Edwards, Betty 6
Edwards, Honeyboy 51
elders 6, 71, 72, 80, 81
Elvis 63
English 11, 25-26, 29-31, 33-35, 38, 82, 103, 106, 120, 130-135, 142
enthusiasm 86, 87
exercises 92, 93, 95-97, 99-101, 104-106, 111, 119, 130, 136-141

F

Faithful, Marianne 74
Father of the Blues 52
fear 5, 8, 31, 73, 74, 77, 79, 84, 122
Fee, Liz 59, 73, 80, 85
Fitzgerald, Ella 29
Flagstad, Kirsten 42, 43, 123
Flanagan, Bill 64
Flesch, Sharon 81
Floyd, Andre 9
focus 5-7, 59, 71, 77-78, 98-100, 103, 109-110, 114, 118-119, 121-122, 137
folk 15, 22, 26, 38-39, 42, 51, 53-54, 57-58, 61-63, 73, 75, 80, 82, 85, 143
Folk City 63, 64
Foster, Stephen 48
French 26-28, 33, 59, 74, 131, 134, 135
Friedman, Judith 80

G

Gavoty, Bernard 27
German 20-21, 26-27, 29, 33, 46, 61, 69, 74, 106, 127, 129-131
Gingras, Louie 72
Gobbi, Titi 46
Gooding, Cynthia 53
Grace, Tony 54

Great Falls, Montana 10
Grey, Zane 54
Grisman, David 41
Gulezian, Michael 11

H

habit 7, 15, 23, 27, 35, 36, 70, 71, 72, 118, 135
Hahn, Reynaldo 24, 26, 59, 109, 120, 122
Handel 38, 44
Handy, William 51, 52
heart 9-11, 16, 21, 33, 36, 41, 46, 49, 51, 54, 56-57, 60-62,
    68, 72-73, 75, 78-79, 134
Hidatsa 22
Hill, Billy 54
Hot Springs, Montana 3, 7, 22
Howard University 49
Hughes, Joe 62

I

imagery 78, 98, 108, 115
improvisation 78, 79
inflection 31, 34, 39, 102
inner critic 68, 72, 78
Italian 3, 7, 19-20, 22-24, 26-27, 29-30, 33, 41-42, 45, 47,
    53, 63, 74, 76-77, 82-83, 90, 94, 106, 109, 115, 127,
    130-131, 142
Italy 20, 44, 45, 46

J

Jacobs-Bonds, Carrie 51
Judy, Stephanie 79

K

Keillor, Garrison 22
Kipnis, Alexander 46
Knowles, Robert 19
Kootenai 19, 72
Korn, Michael 8
Kretschmar, Susan 83, 84

Pisano, Nicki 5, 7, 15
pitch 91, 100, 103, 106, 108-110, 114, 119-122
placement 98-100, 109, 113
Plains, Montana 85
Pons, Lily 44, 80, 45
Ponselle, Rosa 3, 42, 73, 88
pop music 48, 63
Porco, Mike 63
Prairie Home Companion 8
Proctor, Donald 21, 23
pronunciation 102, 104, 106, 113, 115, 119-121, 130, 132, 134-135

R

Raitt, Bonnie 61
ranges 124, 126, 128, 129, 142, 143
register 109, 110, 112, 127, 129
resonance 99, 100, 103, 112, 113, 119
right-brained 6
Ristad, Eloise 67, 68, 73, 76, 77, 78, 79
rock and roll 50

S

Salish 19, 76
schools 23, 30, 83, 86
Schumann-Heink, Ernestine 42
Seeger, Pete 63
Seeger, Tony 30
self discovery 12
Shakespeare, William 22, 120
Shelton, Robert 63
silent movies 52
soft palate 98, 103, 109, 122
songbag 48, 57, 60
Spanish 27, 45
speech 102, 103, 106, 120, 124, 130

spontaneity 67

stage fright 71, 122

Swedish nightingale 43

T

talent 13, 20, 21, 49, 67, 68, 83

tempo 36, 76

tension 15, 99, 118-122, 126

Tetrazzini, Luisa 42, 45

The Bond Shop 51

Thompson Falls, Montana 32, 75, 77

throat 91, 94, 98, 100, 112-114, 118, 121, 127, 130, 132

timbre 129

Tinsley, Jim Bob 54, 57

tone 91-92, 94-95, 97-100, 103, 106, 108-115, 118-122,
    127, 129-130, 134, 137

tongue 91, 94, 98-99, 102-103, 112-113, 118, 120-122, 130,
    133, 134-135

Toscanini, Arturo 47

trail song 55, 56, 57, 61

Travers, Mary 47, 63

Triplett, Bonnie Jean 11, 70, 71

Trowbridge, Kenny 8

truth 3, 21, 46, 68, 76

Turner, Eva 44

Turner, Jessica Baron 4, 82, 83

U

Ulrich, Homer 78

University of Montana 22, 23, 26, 78

Uris, Dorothy 30, 102, 120

V

Van, Dave Ronk 15

Villa, Valentina 47

vocal cord 91, 94

vocal cords 114, 120, 125

vocal exercises 92-93, 95-97, 99-101, 104-106, 111, 130, 136-141

vocal timbre 129

voice ranges 126, 142

Von Tilzer 50

vowels 27, 29-30, 35, 78, 81, 104, 106, 120, 130, 134, 136-137

W

Wahl, Art 54

walk 6, 11-15, 31, 36-38, 46, 56, 68, 71, 74, 79

Walker, Alice 53

warm ups 14

work songs 49

Y

yoga 16, 17

Young, Paul 56

Z

Zimmerman, Lee 13, 79